# *Butterflies in the Backyard*

## Scott Shalaway

STACKPOLE
BOOKS

*To the faculty of the University of Delaware's
Department of Entomology and Applied Ecology,
circa 1974—thanks for all the lessons.*

Copyright © 2004 by Scott Shalaway

Published by
STACKPOLE BOOKS
5067 Ritter Road
Mechanicsburg, PA 17055
www.stackpolebooks.com

Printed in the United States of America

10  9  8  7  6  5  4  3  2  1

First edition

*Cover design by Caroline Stover*
*Cover photographs by Richard Day/Daybreak Imagery*
*Photo section credits: All photographs by Richard Day/Daybreak Imagery except for Garden with salvias, asters, petunias, artemisias, and baby's breath, by Susan Day/Daybreak Imagery*

**Library of Congress Cataloging-in-Publication Data**

Shalaway, Scott.
  Butterflies in the backyard / Scott Shalaway.—1st ed.
     p. cm.
  Includes bibliographical references.
  ISBN 0-8117-2695-9
  1. Butterflies. 2. Butterfly gardening. I. Title.
QL542 .S5 2004
595.78—dc22

                                                      2003022283

# Contents

# Acknowledgments

Writing a book is hard work, but the day of publication always makes it all worthwhile. My sincere thanks to all who played a part—Stackpole editor Mark Allison, Doug Tallamy, John Rawlins, anonymous copy editors, and especially my wife, Linda, for her support, encouragement, and sharp red pencil.

# Introduction

If you love to see butterflies in your backyard, if you marvel at the giant silkworm moths that gather at your porch lights on summer nights, if you're fascinated by the countless caterpillars you find in your garden or on your shade trees, this book is for you. I've called upon my thirty years of experience as a naturalist and a seldom used B.S. degree in entomology from the University of Delaware to explain the natural history of the most common members of the order Lepidoptera (from the Greek *lepis,* meaning "scale," and *ptera,* "wing") that we all see in our backyards or on the back forty.

The ancient Greeks had it right. Their word for butterfly was *psyche,* which was also their word for the soul. They recognized that adult butterflies emerge, or are reborn, after passing through what they considered a deathlike pupal stage.

Though many insect life cycles include complete metamorphosis, butterflies and moths, members of the order Lepidoptera, a subunit of the invertebrate class Insecta, are the ones we notice most often. And unlike our attitude toward many insects, we usually appreciate them rather than try to kill them.

Butterflies, in particular, catch our fancy. They are colorful, active by day, and frequent visitors to our backyards and gardens. And unlike many birds, which share these appealing characteristics, butterflies don't rise at the crack of dawn. They rely on the morning sun to warm them up, so butterflies usually wait until midmorning to become active. That means butterfly-watchers, unlike birders, can sleep in.

Have you ever known anyone to hate butterflies? Neither have I. Some gardeners don't appreciate the caterpillars—the larval stage—but they still love the adult butterflies as they flutter by. And butterflies pollinate many plants, thus performing an invaluable ecological service.

To appreciate the biological significance of insects, and by extension lepidopterans, let's examine the earth's biodiversity and put the lepidopterans in perspective. This is a risky business at best, because few biologists agree on such numbers, but I'll use Harvard entomologist Edward O. Wilson as my authority. In *The Diversity of Life* (1992, Harvard University Press), Wilson estimates the total number of known species of living organisms to be 1,413,000. He also points out that evolutionary biologists agree that this is less than one-tenth the number of species that actually inhabit the planet. Generations of future biologists will be kept busy just finding and naming new species.

Of those 1.4 million known species, 751,000, or 53.1 percent, are insects. Other major or easily recognized groups include algae (26,900; 1.9 percent), fungi (69,000; 4.9 percent), higher plants (248,400; 17.5 percent), mollusks (50,000; 3.5 percent), fish (18,800; 1.3 percent), amphibians (4,200; 0.30 percent), reptiles (6,300; 0.45 percent), birds (9,000; 0.64 percent), and mammals (4,000; 0.28 percent).

Insects' dominance of the planet's biodiversity is apparent. More than half of all species are insects. And most of those are beetles (290,000; 20.5 percent of all living species). The next largest insect group is Lepidoptera (140,000 species; 9.9 percent). And of the lepidopterans, most (125,500; 89.6 percent) are moths. That leaves about 14,500 species of butterflies, of which approximately 760 occur in North America north of Mexico. (Coincidentally, this is approximately the same number of bird species found in North America.) More than 6,000 species of butterflies are found in the American tropics.

Curiously, butterflies and moths are not formally recognized as distinct taxonomic groups by entomologists. But then, taxonomists are a curious breed that seldom agree on much of anything. What is agreed on, however, is that butterflies and skippers are relatively recent groups descended from moths. The ability to exploit the diurnal environment may be what originally sparked the evolution of this most familiar group of insects.

Despite the ambiguity of differences between butterflies and moths, they can be lumped into three groups based on some general traits. Most butterflies are active by day, have a club or swollen tip at the end of the antennae, and hold their wings vertically over the body at rest. Skippers, more butterfly than moth, have a distinctive hook at the tip of the antennae, fly by day, and hold their wings like butterflies. Moths are primarily nocturnal and have pointed antennae that may be feathery or threadlike but lack a swollen or hooked tip, and most perch with their wings held flat at rest.

Despite the beautiful color photos found in this book, it is not a field guide. The Further Reading section includes a list of my favorite field guides, and there are many good ones. This book is more a celebration of the fascinating natural history of common butterflies and moths. It introduces you to some of North America's most common lepidopteran species, explores the mysteries of metamorphosis and Monarch migration, and teaches you how to attract more butterflies to your backyard and garden. A basic understanding of the natural history of common species provides a solid foundation for additional study. If you're ready for a better understanding of this often beautiful and always fascinating group of insects, read on.

# CHAPTER 1

# Lepidopteran Biology

A life cycle defined by complete metamorphosis from egg, to larva, to pupa, to adult makes the study of butterflies and moths a fascinating journey. Let's begin with a brief look at each stage of the life cycle and continue through other aspects of lepidopteran biology that can be appreciated in the backyard as well as in a wilderness area.

## LIFE CYCLE

**The Egg.** A butterfly or moth begins life as an egg, and as might be expected, these eggs are tiny, usually 1 to 2 millimeters. Most are oval but flat on each end, like miniature barrels. Under a hand lens, the egg walls appear ribbed. Eggs are typically laid on the tops or bottoms of plant leaves, or sometimes on stems.

Within the egg, the embryonic caterpillar grows quickly. Many species spend only about a week in the egg, but some overwinter as eggs. These lie dormant during the fall and winter months. Whenever development begins, the embryo grows quickly into a tiny larva, which ultimately eats its way out of the egg.

**The Larva.** Upon emergence, the tiny larva, which we know as a caterpillar, eats voraciously and grows rapidly. Caterpillars are soft-bodied, and many are covered with protective hairs or spines. Small eyes, tiny antennae, and massive jaws, called mandibles, are found on the head, which is composed of hard keratinized material similar to your fingernails. Sturdy mandibles are necessary to chew tough plant material.

A caterpillar's elongate body seems dominated by legs, of which there are two types. The forward three pairs are jointed, located on the thorax, and homologous to those found on adults. Behind these true legs, on the abdomen, are five pairs of prolegs. On the tip of each proleg is a ring of tiny, hooklike structures called crochets. These act almost like suction cups, grasping leaves and twigs as the caterpillars move. Changes in blood pressure cause the prolegs to grip and release objects as they move. The progressive action of the prolegs gives caterpillars their distinctive undulating form of locomotion.

The primary purpose of the larval stage is to eat and grow. Caterpillars are eating machines. Surprisingly, though, most are quite selective in their eating habits. Many species eat the leaves of a single plant species or specialize on a group of closely related species. So the key to attracting butterflies to any backyard is to provide the species of plants preferred by the caterpillars of the butterflies you wish to attract. Monarch caterpillars, for example, eat only milkweeds, so if you want Monarchs reproducing in your backyard, you need to have some milkweed in your garden.

Why most caterpillars are so inflexibly host-specific is a fascinating story of the coevolution of plants and insects. Over the eons, insects have waged constant war on plants. Plants responded by developing a variety of protective measures. Some developed thick, heavy leaves that are difficult to eat. Others have thorns, spines, or dense mats of hair. Still others produce toxins that make them distasteful to most herbivores. Plant species that failed to adapt to herbivorous insects went extinct.

The ecological struggle between plants and insects has left us with a planet populated by many specialized species. Milkweeds, for example, in order to survive the constant onslaught of plant-eating insects, evolved a distasteful chemical that repels most insects. Monarch butterfly larvae and those of related species, however, have evolved the ability to harmlessly incorporate these chemicals into their body tissues. But when a predator attempts to eat a Monarch caterpillar, it is repulsed by the presence of the chemical in the caterpillar's flesh. This is just one example of the thousands of complex ecological relationships that have evolved between plants and lepidopteran larvae.

Metamorphosis, the transition from larva to pupa to adult, is accomplished through molting, a process in which the caterpillar sheds its skin. Caterpillars molt three to five times, each time emerging as a larger caterpillar. This is why caterpillars are not found in an infinite range of ever-increasing sizes. As they grow, the joints between body segments stretch, and a new, larger exoskeleton forms inside the old one. When it's time for the next larval stage, each of which is called an instar, the caterpillar gulps air and inflates. This forces the old exoskeleton to split, and the new larval instar crawls out of its old skin. Pupae and adults emerge from their previous form in a similar manner.

Transforming changes have already begun inside the growing larvae. Wings and some major organs arise from cells present in maturing larvae. These transformations accelerate during the last forty-eight hours of the final instar stage.

**The Pupa.** When the final larval instar is ready to pupate, signaled by hormonal changes, it stops eating and allows its digestive system to empty. Then it wanders until it finds a suitable pupation site. Depending on the species, that may be on a twig, inside a rolled-up leaf, amidst the leaf litter, or underground. Many caterpillars spin silk to attach themselves to their selected perches. Some, such as swallowtails, spin a silk girdle around the midsection. Others, like Monarchs, spin a silk pad and suspend themselves upside down. Still others may remain in their larval leaf nest (skippers) or spin a few threads of silk around some leaves to form a shelter (some satyrs). Some simply pupate underground.

To initiate pupation, the larva wriggles out of its final caterpillar skin to emerge as a pupa. A butterfly pupa is called a chrysalis, and a moth pupa is known as a cocoon.

Though a chrysalis or cocoon is commonly referred to as a resting stage in the life cycle, the pupal stage is far from quiescent, except for those species that overwinter in this form. For a week to ten days after pupation, fantastic physiological changes take place within the pupa. The musculature is reorganized for flight, and sperm and eggs mature.

All of these miraculous changes are triggered and controlled by chemical hormones within the organism's body. Textbooks have been written to completely describe the phenomenon of metamorphosis, yet even now our understanding of it is incomplete. But we can certainly shake our heads in wonder.

The skin of some chrysalises is translucent and becomes remarkably clear as the pupal period proceeds. An increasingly popular science project in elementary schools is to capture Monarch caterpillars and observe metamorphosis. As the pupa matures, the colorful orange and black butterfly wings become visible through the translucent skin of the chrysalis. Every elementary student should witness this at least once, because the process of metamorphosis instills in students a wonder of nature that books and lectures simply cannot provide.

**The Adult.** When the adult is fully developed, the pupal case splits, and the adult butterfly emerges. It crawls to a nearby perch and pumps blood into its crinkled wings. It may take several hours for the wings to unfurl and harden, during which time the adult is vulnerable to predators. As soon as the wings harden, the adult flies off in search of a mate to fulfill its primary mission, which is to reproduce. When a female lays her first clutch of fertilized eggs, the life cycle is complete.

Some adults migrate to escape harsh winter weather, such as the Monarchs, and others hibernate, such as the Mourning Cloaks, but most adults live a short life whose sole purpose is to procreate. Some butterflies and many moths have nonfunctional mouthparts and do not even eat during their final stage of life.

Like all insects, an adult lepidopteran has a head with two antennae, a thorax to which six legs and four wings are attached, and an elongate abdomen. In place of the caterpillar's powerful chewing mandibles, the adult has tubular mouthparts that remain coiled beneath the head except when being used. When extended, the strawlike proboscis is used to sip nectar and other fluids. In addition to nectar, some butterflies drink a variety of other liquid foods, probing sap wells, rotting fruit, aphid honeydew, mud, dung, or carrion for sugar or minerals. It is sometimes amazing where nutrition and energy can be found in nature.

Flower nectar is roughly 20 percent sugar, and it is the energy in that sugar that fuels the reproductive effort of most butterflies. Mating usually takes place shortly after adults emerge from their chrysalises, and females lay most of their eggs within a few days of emergence. Then they die, and the fate of the species lies in the eggs of the next generation.

Among the larger, more spectacular giant silkworm moths, such as Lunas and Cecropias, which lack functional mouthparts, the short-lived adults rely on energy reserves passed on through the pupal stage. Many other moths also do not feed as adults.

Perhaps the most distinctive characteristic of both butterflies and moths, and one that is often overlooked until they are handled, is the scales that cover the body. If you handle a butterfly, invariably some rub off onto your fingers. Lepidopteran scales serve the same functions as feathers do for birds. They give the insects their color, help insulate them from the cold, and improve the aerodynamics of the wings. Without scales, there would be no butterflies or moths as we know them.

Another anatomical feature that lepidopterans share with other insects is that the body lacks internal bones and is supported by an exoskeleton, a system of hard, rigid, external plates. The exoskeleton offers protection, reduces water loss, and provides an almost unlimited number of points for muscle attachment. This is an ideal system of structural support for relatively small creatures.

## LIFE SPAN

Most butterflies and moths have a short life span. Some moths live only a few days, some butterflies only a week or two. For any given species, the life span is relatively fixed, dictated primarily by climate. Many arctic and alpine species require two years to complete their life cycle, as there simply isn't enough time to go through all four stages in a single season. In the boreal forest across most of Canada, most lepidopterans raise one brood per year. In temperate zones, two generations are typical. Across the southern tier of states, three broods per year are not uncommon. And in the tropics, adults may breed all year. Warmer climates permit a longer growing season for plants, and insects in general grow faster in warmer climates.

## OVERWINTERING STRATEGIES

In most of the United States, lepidopterans must somehow deal with cold winter temperatures. Most enter a winter diapause, more commonly known as hibernation or overwintering. Diapause is a general term used to describe a dormant period during which an organism survives unfavorable weather. Summer diapause, which can be triggered by a predictable dry season, is called estivation and is most common among tropical species.

Some species overwinter as eggs, some as a particular larval instar, some as pupae, and a few as adults. Gypsy Moths, Eastern Tent Caterpillars, and most coppers overwinter as eggs; skippers and Woolly Bears hibernate as larvae; swallowtails and silk moths hibernate as pupae; Mourning Cloaks and anglewings hibernate as adults in hollow trees or behind loose slabs of bark on dead and dying trees, emerging on unseasonably warm winter days and going back into their winter refuges when the cold returns. A few species migrate great distances from north to south to escape winter weather. The Monarch is the most famous winter migrant, and science only learned the details of this migration in the 1970s.

The internal biological clock that controls diapause is set to photoperiod. Shorter days signal lepidopterans that it's time to while away the winter. After a period of cold winter weather, their internal clocks detect the lengthening days of spring and activity resumes: Eggs hatch, larvae feed and pupate, and adults emerge from pupal cases.

## SENSORY PERCEPTION

Butterflies are visual creatures, with huge compound eyes composed of hundreds of tiny eyes called ommatidia. Though they don't see things as we do, they are capable of seeing all the colors of the spectrum from red through violet and can easily detect movement. This makes finding other butterflies in flight and colorful flowers blowing in the wind relatively easy.

Even more important than vision to butterflies are the senses of smell and taste. Though pores sensitive to smell are scattered all over a butterfly's body, the primary olfactory organs are the antennae. Taste buds are found on the antennae, proboscis, and legs. The taste sensors on the legs are probably the most important in butterflies, as females identify host plants by tasting them with their legs. A female Monarch, for example, recognizes a milkweed plant by the chemical messages she gets through her legs.

When a female butterfly searches for a host plant upon which to lay her eggs, she drums her forelegs against the leaf surface she lands on. Tiny spines on her legs pierce the plant, and sensitive olfactory hairs on the legs "taste" the fluids that flow from the wound. If she's on the appropriate species, she lays some eggs on the leaves. If not, she moves on.

Moths, on the other hand, are primarily nocturnal and rely most on a keen sense of smell. Those with large, feathery antennae, such as Lunas and Cecropias, are particularly dependent on their antennae's sense of smell. Because they are short-lived and usually not terribly abundant, these moths need an efficient way to find each other to mate before they die. Females release chemicals called pheromones, which males can detect up to a mile away. Thanks to their odor-detecting antennae, male moths can detect and find females over relatively great distances.

Some moths mate throughout the night, but many mate during a particular time period. Because females "call" males with their pheromones, these mating hours are known as the "calling time." Cecropia moths, for example, call from 3 A.M. to sunrise.

## DAILY BEHAVIOR

Like all insects, butterflies are ectothermic; that is, their body temperature changes with the environment's temperature. Most butterflies are active between 60 and 108 degrees Fahrenheit. In the morning, they warm themselves by spreading their wings and basking in the sun. Often they perch on sun-baked rocks or soil. That's why butterfly-watchers needn't rise at the crack of dawn like birders. If butterflies get too hot in the afternoon, they close their wings or fly to shady spots.

During daylight hours, butterflies spend most of their time searching for mates and sipping nectar. After mating, females devote most of their time to finding host plants and laying eggs.

At the end of the day, butterflies roost on the tops of trees and shrubs. Most roost singly and often cling to the undersides of leaves, which offers some protection from wind and rain.

## MATING

Butterflies search for mates in two ways: perching or patrolling. Perching behavior reminds me of spring break at the beach. Male butterflies visit favorite perches at particular times. Certain species prefer certain perches, such as hilltops, rocks, or treetops. When a moving object catches a male's attention, he flies out to determine if it is a female of his own species. If it is, he mates. If not, he returns to the perch. Sometimes butterflies appear to be chasing the wrong species, other insects, or even people, but they are simply searching for females of the right species. Butterfly vision is better at detecting fluttering movements and colors than specific objects, so they check out all potential mates. The Painted Lady is an example of a perching species.

Patrolling behavior is a bit different. It's more like cruising for chicks. Males fly almost continuously in search of females. When they meet, they mate. Monarchs are patrollers.

Males and females identify each other by using a variety of cues. Flight pattern, wing color, and odor all can be used to determine if males and females are of the same species.

When males and females meet, mating behavior can range from simple to complex, and this varies from species to species. This is relatively easy to observe, so ambitious butterfly-watchers can learn many details of their favorites species' behavior simply by watching.

Sometimes mating is quick and without any ritual. Other times pairs engage in ritualized aerial dancing. Some flutter next to each other, brush each other's wings, or tap antennae. The actual act of mating lasts from minutes to hours, with mating time directly related to the size of the butterfly. Larger species take more time to mate. The purpose of all mating behavior, no matter how simple or complex, is to be sure that both individuals are members of the same species.

Upon emerging from the chrysalis, a female's eggs are mature, and she can mate immediately. Some females mate with several males; others mate only once. Males can mate many times, but most must mature for about a day after emerging.

After mating, females must find suitable host plants upon which to lay her eggs, or oviposit. A female ready to oviposit flies slowly and deliberately over the landscape, searching for host plants. She lands on many plants, drumming on the leaves with her forelegs to taste them. If it's not the right plant, she continues her flight. When she finds a host plant, she takes her time. Most butterflies lay eggs singly or in small clusters, gluing them to a leaf or stem. Usually eggs are deposited on the underside of a leaf. After laying an egg, the female moves to another leaf or another plant. Over the course of their brief lives, most female butterflies lay hundreds of eggs.

## MIGRATION

Most butterflies are fairly sedentary, completing their entire life cycle within a relatively small area. But a few butterflies complete annual migrations that rival those of migratory birds.

Migratory species produce at least several generations per year, and they overwinter in the south. Only one generation migrates each way, so the most amazing part of butterfly migration is simply how they do it. These are insects with brains no bigger than a pinhead. And yet the final summer generation of butterflies somehow knows when and where to go for the winter. In North America, the grandest migrants are Monarch and Painted Ladies.

During migration, butterflies seem single-minded. They can fly in a constant direction at about 30 miles per hour all day long. They fly over trees and houses, rather than around them. I was at a football game at the University of Delaware stadium in the early 1970s, when a stream of Monarchs passed over the highest bleachers for more than an hour. The sight was more compelling to a young entomology student than anything taking place on the field.

Exactly how migrating butterflies maintain a constant direction is uncertain. Because butterflies do not travel on cloudy, rainy days, they probably use the position of the sun as it crosses the sky. They are also known to use landmarks. And because Monarchs and Red Admirals have been observed migrating at night, they probably can use the stars and moon to navigate as well. But how do they know where they are and, more important, where they are going? Clearly migrant butterflies have some sort of map genetically imprinted on their brains.

## AVOIDING PREDATION

Some butterflies and caterpillars avoid predation by being poisonous to vertebrate predators. If birds or mice eat these butterflies or caterpillars, they quickly get violently ill and vomit. Not wanting to repeat such trauma, they learn quickly to avoid those particular butterflies and caterpillars.

Poisonous species either pick up the toxins from host plants as caterpillars or make their own. Monarch caterpillars eat milkweeds, which contain heart poisons known as cardiac glycerides. The poisonous chemicals are retained by the pupal and adult stages, so Monarchs are not bothered by many predators. Predators also avoid Viceroy butterflies, which do not eat milkweeds and are not poisonous, because they look like Monarchs. Both are burnt orange with distinctive black striping patterns. This is an example of Batesian mimicry, where the edible mimic looks like the poisonous model.

The look-alike Monarch and Queen caterpillars, closely related members of the genus *Danaus,* are Mullerian mimics. They both eat toxic milkweeds and both are poisonous. This benefits both species, because predators only have to eat one to learn to avoid them both. If the caterpillars were distinguishable, predators would have to learn to avoid each, at the cost of more dead caterpillars. The value of Mullerian mimicry may not be as apparent as Batesian mimicry, but it is measurable.

Recent evidence suggests that Viceroys may also be Mullerian mimics in southern parts of their range. In parts of Florida, Viceroy caterpillars eat toxic plants, and the poisonous chemicals are incorporated into their body tissues. So depending on geography, Viceroys may or may not be toxic to predators, but they are always examples of either Batesian or Mullerian mimicry.

Some poisonous species manufacture their own toxins. When disturbed or bothered by predators, swallowtail caterpillars evert a structure called an osmeterium from the first segment of the thorax. This is a forked, malodorous, fleshy gland sometimes referred to as a "snake tongue" because of its appearance. Its odor, and perhaps its appearance, repels ants and other predators.

Not all mimics involve poisonous chemicals. Some swallowtail caterpillars have eyespots that resemble snakes' eyes, and some butterflies and moths have eyespots on their wings that suggest an owl's face when revealed. These ruses may not seem terribly convincing to us, but a bird might decide it's safer to eat positively identifiable prey rather than risk attacking something that might attack back. Or maybe that fraction of a second the predator hesitates when encountering a mimic is just enough to provide time to escape, at least occasionally.

Many cryptically colored butterflies and moths resemble dead leaves. Some caterpillars mimic twigs. And some caterpillars, pupal cases, and even adult moths mimic bird droppings. In fact there's an entire group of North American species called bird dropping moths.

## CHAPTER 2

# Close-ups

Certain species of butterflies and moths enjoy a level of familiarity to anyone who spends much time in the backyard. Gardeners and birders, in particular, encounter a few butterflies, moths, and caterpillars on a fairly regular basis. The following series of brief essays describes some interesting aspects of the natural history of some of these species.

## SWALLOWTAILS

Though the world's largest and most spectacular butterflies live in the tropics of South America, Africa, and New Guinea, North America's showiest species are the swallowtails, members of the family Papilionidae. Though only 30 of the world's 560 species of swallowtails occur in North America, the distributions of the Canadian Tiger Swallowtail and the Artemisia Swallowtail reach well into the interior of Alaska.

Swallowtails typically are large and brightly colored, and most have short "tails" extending from the ends of their hind wings. A unique behavioral characteristic also helps identify the swallowtails. Most butterflies perch quietly while feeding, but swallowtails stay aloft while nectaring by fluttering their wings. Because swallowtails are so large, perhaps they "flutter feed" so they won't cause the flowers to tilt to the ground.

Among the most common and widespread swallowtails are the Black Swallowtail and Tiger Swallowtail. Black Swallowtails occur east of the Rocky Mountains through the United States and southern Canada. Tiger Swallowtails occupy all but the most northern reaches of the continent.

Black Swallowtails should be familiar to most vegetable gardeners, because their host plants are members of the carrot family (Umbelliferae). Look for caterpillars on the leaves of carrot, celery, parsley, parsnip, anise, dill, fennel, cumin, and coriander. The young caterpillar is black with a white, saddlelike marking near the center. It actually mimics a bird dropping. After the third larval molt, the caterpillar is green with yellow-dotted black stripes. Why the caterpillar makes such a drastic change in appearance is unclear, but it always has its osmeterium for defense.

After the fifth larval molt, the chrysalis emerges. Pupae formed in the summer are green; those formed in the fall are brown. In both cases, the chrysalis matches the surrounding vegetation. After overwintering as a chrysalis, as all swallowtails do, new Black Swallowtails emerge in the spring with just one thing on their tiny minds—reproduction.

Males emerge a few days before females and establish territories on hilltops. After territories are established, Black Swallowtails defend them aggressively. They drive away trespassing males and are even known to chase black birds and darkly clothed entomologists. Perhaps this is the source of the phrase "king of the hill."

Tiger Swallowtails are one of the most common species in my West Virginia backyard. They first appear in April, and the population peaks in July and August, when clouds of them descend on blooming joe-pye weed. Midsummer congregations of Tiger Swallowtails "puddle" along local streams for drinks of water and gather on fresh cow manure and patches of various types of animal urine to sip up minerals left behind.

Like young Black Swallowtail caterpillars, young Tiger larvae resemble bird droppings. But older Tiger larval instars are large, green, and fleshy, with prominent eyespots that give them an ominous snakelike appearance. This threatening aspect combined with the foul-smelling osmeterium protect Tiger caterpillars from most predators.

Though Tiger Swallowtails are typically bright yellow with black stripes and easy to recognize, in the southern part of their range as many as 95 percent of females are almost entirely black. This mimics the appearance of Pipevine Swallowtails, which are distasteful because their caterpillars eat Dutchman's pipe and related species in the genus *Aristolochia*. These plants contain noxious chemicals, which are incorporated into the caterpillars' tissues and are passed along to the adult butterflies. So even though black female Tiger Swallowtails are quite tasty, mammalian, avian, and even insect predators avoid them because they've learned that black butterflies taste terrible. Populations of Black Swallowtails and Spicebush Swallowtails whose ranges overlap with Pipevine Swallowtails enjoy the same protection.

## PAINTED LADIES

If swallowtails are the most glamorous butterflies in North America, the Painted Ladies (*Vanessa cardui*) are the most ubiquitous. In fact, they are known to occur on every continent except Antarctica. So whether you're in Illinois, Costa Rica, Germany, Vietnam, New Zealand, or Australia, you're likely to encounter this pretty little lady. It is truly a cosmopolitan species and is sometimes called the Cosmopolitan Butterfly.

One reason Painted Ladies are so widespread is that the host plants their caterpillars require are also cosmopolitan species. Thistles are Lady caterpillar favorites, and other hosts include cocklebur, burdock, yarrow, and pussytoes. Because of the Painted Lady's taste for thistles, it is a favorite of farmers in parts of the country where non-native thistles have become invasive pests. This is a caterpillar that can do the job of expensive herbicides at no cost. If more farmers and land managers had a better understanding of butterfly biology in general, and Painted Ladies in particular, there would be no limit to their popularity.

Painted Ladies lay eggs singly on the tops of host leaves. The caterpillars range from yellow or lavender to brownish gray and are protected by many yellow, orange, and/or black branched spines. The body segments are separated by many narrow yellow vertical lines, and a yellow stripe runs along each side of the body. Painted Lady caterpillars pull together pieces of leaves and buds and use their own silk to build little nests on top of the leaves. Then they eat the leaves within, move on, and build another nest. After several instars, they pupate and transform into adult Ladies.

Painted Ladies overwinter as adults, but they cannot survive cold winters. So each spring, Painted Ladies emerge at southern latitudes, and as their population builds and host food becomes scarce, they head north to repopulate areas where it's too cold to overwinter. In this sense, Ladies can be considered migratory, though they make only a one-way flight rather than a true migration.

American Painted Ladies (*Vanessa virginiensis*) are a related and similar species found across the United States and southern Canada. Though it strays to South America and even across the Atlantic Ocean, it is not nearly as widespread as its cousin. Like the Painted Lady, American Ladies overwinter as adults and disperse northward as the summer populations grow.

The America Lady caterpillar is similar to the Painted Lady, though more colorful. Yellow-green stripes separate each segment, and bands of red and white spots run the length of the body.

The Red Admiral (*Vanessa atalanta*) is another widespread member of this genus that should be familiar to many nature watchers. It ranges from the edge of the arctic tundra to subtropical zones in the Western Hemisphere and is also native to North Africa, Eurasia, and New Zealand.

Like the Ladies, Red Admirals lay single eggs on the tops of host leaves, in this case, stinging nettles. Red Admiral caterpillars also build silk nests around their food source, but they take the construction a bit further. An older caterpillar will chew into the leaf stem, causing the edges of the leaf to droop. It then weaves the edges of the leaves together and lives inside the leaf tube, which it eventually consumes.

## RED-SPOTTED PURPLE/WHITE ADMIRAL

In the animal world, some species occur in two or more distinct forms, such as Snow and Blue Geese and the red and gray phases of screech-owls. Among butterflies, Red-Spotted Purples and White Admirals are classified as the single species *Limenitis arthemis*. The species occurs throughout the eastern United States and most of Canada. Throughout the mid-Atlantic and Great Lakes states, both forms occur, freely interbreed, and produce healthy, fertile offspring. Red-Spotted Purples dominate south of this zone of overlap; White Admirals occur to the north. In my West Virginia backyard, Purples are common, and I've never seen a White Admiral.

White Admirals and Purples lay eggs singly on the leaves of a variety of common trees, including willow, poplar, birch, cherry, apple, hawthorn, elm, oak, and beech. Third-instar caterpillars hibernate in protected areas and emerge in the spring. Adults eat a wide range of foods, including nectar, sap, fruit, carrion, dung, honeydew, and even decaying wood.

## MONARCHS

As I walked along the beach in Cape May, New Jersey, migration was on my mind. It was early, August 10 to be exact, but already shorebirds had begun passing through. Sanderlings played tag with the waves, Ruddy Turnstones rested on the beach, and Least Sandpipers flew up and down the shore. Great Egrets passed overhead in groups of two or three, perhaps on their way to Delaware. And a lone Brown Pelican sailed south along the coast.

On the sand dunes just 100 yards from the ocean, another, more subtle migration was under way. A steady stream of Monarch butterflies fluttered by. Some stopped periodically to sip nectar from the many colorful wildflowers that dot the dunes. Their passage reminded me that birds are not the only animals that migrate. Monarchs (*Danaus plexippus*) are equally renowned for their annual long-distance movements.

Each summer and fall, these colorful orange and black insects migrate south for the winter. Western populations winter along the Southern California coast; Monarchs east of the Rockies migrate to the Gulf Coast or central Mexico. Mark and recapture studies have shown that Monarchs travel as far as 1,800 miles in just four months. They move only by day, at a leisurely pace of 5 to 18 mph.

Not only do Monarchs travel great distances, but they do so with unerring accuracy. Year after year, they return to the same wintering areas, even the same trees. So reliable are these migratory aggregations that they have become major tourist attractions in Mexico and Southern California. The town of Pacific Grove, California, proudly calls itself "Butterfly City, U.S.A."

What makes the Monarch migration even more amazing is that each butterfly makes the trip only once. Monarchs that return in the spring lay eggs, then die. Consequently, one to several generations of Monarchs separate those that return in the spring from those that depart in the fall. Yet somehow each fall, inexperienced Monarchs return to their ancestors' traditional wintering areas. Some researchers suggest that genetic olfactory cues could provide the guidance.

On their winter grounds, Monarchs are sluggish and inactive. They congregate on tree trunks by the millions. Imagine so many butterflies on a tree limb that it snaps under their weight. It happens.

During the winter, the Monarchs use very little of their fat reserves. By February, they still have plenty of stored energy for the trip north. Mating occurs before migration begins, and females lay eggs as they move northward. After reaching the southern states, eastern Monarchs, which have lived as long as eight months, die. But the eggs they have left behind ensure a new generation of Monarchs as far as the females survived. This new generation continues northward, laying eggs as it goes, until three or four generations later, adult Monarchs reach the northern limits of milkweed distribution. Individuals from these summer broods live only three to five weeks, just long enough to reproduce. The final summer brood is the one that will return to the mountains of Mexico. Populations west of the Rockies winter in Southern California and will go through at least two generations during migration.

Female Monarchs lay pinhead-size eggs on the undersides of leaves of milkweed plants. In three to twelve days, the eggs hatch and tiny, ravenous caterpillars emerge. Bold black, white, and yellow rings encircle the body and identify the fleshy larval stage. Within fourteen days, they devour enough milkweed leaves to weigh more than two thousand times their hatching weight.

Each caterpillar then finds a protected perch and molts into a pupal case, called a chrysalis. Over the next two to three weeks, the contents of the pale green, gold-flecked chrysalis transform from a lowly caterpillar into a beautiful burnt orange and black adult butterfly.

Beautiful as they may be, most Monarch larvae and adults are foul-tasting to most predators. In laboratory experiments, Blue Jays vomit within minutes of eating a Monarch. Why? Because Monarchs are what they eat. Many species of milkweed are highly toxic. Though Monarchs are unaffected by the toxin, they incorporate the poison into their body tissues. The poison is retained through metamorphosis, so that even the adults have high concentrations.

Curiously, the toxin is more highly concentrated in the wings and exoskeleton than in the body. Thus a predator that nips even a piece of wing discovers that Monarchs are distasteful. As an added protection, the Monarch's abdomen, like that of many other distasteful species, is tough and leathery, difficult for a predator to bite. These adaptations enable predators to learn that Monarchs taste bad without necessarily killing the butterflies. This also explains why we often see Monarchs with badly battered wings—they are battle scars from the ongoing struggle between predator and prey.

Despite their natural protection, wintering Monarchs do have a few enemies. On the Mexican wintering grounds, Black-Headed Grosbeaks have developed an immunity to these toxins, and Black-Backed Orioles have learned to peel off the butterflies' noxious exoskeletons and eat the soft, tasty inner tissue. These two birds may take as much as 15 percent of the wintering Monarch population in some areas.

## SULPHURS

Spend time on a farm, in an overgrown field, or at a wildflower preserve, and you're certain to see sulphur butterflies. Determining exactly which sulphur you see is quite another matter.

The two most common North American species are the Orange Sulphur (*Colias eurytheme*) and the Common Sulphur (*Colias philodice*), and they have parallel life cycles. Caterpillars of both species are green with white lines along the sides. Both require legumes such as alfalfa, vetch, or clover as host plants. And both overwinter in the pupal stage. As adults, these butterflies are yellow to orange with black wing borders. To see them is to wonder if they inspired the term *butterfly*.

To make identification even more confusing, these two species of sulphurs vary greatly in the extent of the black wing border, and both are prone to albinism, so many are white rather than yellow or orange. The butterflies themselves seem almost as easily confused, and hybrids between the two species are common. But there is one aspect of their elaborate courtship behavior that allows them to distinguish one from the other. The scales on the wings of orange sulphurs reflect ultraviolet light; those of the common sulphur do not. Though this may seem of minor consequence to us, because we cannot see ultraviolet light, it makes all the difference in the world to these two sulphurs, because they can. And since the continent has no shortage of these two sulphurs, this simple reproductive isolating mechanism obviously works.

## MOURNING CLOAKS

Though the appearance of butterflies might seem a reliable harbinger of spring, Mourning Cloaks (*Nymphalis antiopa*) always rush the season. On the first mild day in January, even if a blanket of snow covers the ground, Mourning Cloaks emerge from tree cavities, leaf litter, or behind large slabs of loose bark.

The obvious question about butterflies that emerge on warm winter days is, what do they eat? There are no flowers, and thus no nectar available, in midwinter. Mourning Cloaks actually prefer rotting fruit, animal dung, carrion, and sap. They love fallen apples that deer have overlooked, and piles of fresh excrement are a real treat. If their tiny brains permitted it, they'd revel over roadkill. And though the wells drilled by sapsuckers may madden homeowners, the sap flow that results nourishes not only the sapsuckers, but also winter butterflies.

Because Mourning Cloaks become active so early, they lay eggs in both the spring and late summer. Females lay clusters of eggs around the twigs of elm, poplar, and willow. Unlike most butterfly eggs, which are round or oval, individual Mourning Cloak eggs are many-sided. Perhaps seven- and eight-sided eggs allow the clusters to be packed the most efficiently.

When the eggs hatch, the caterpillars live a communal life. They line up side by side along the leaf margin and eat as a group. If bothered by an ant or other insect, the caterpillars rear up on their hind legs to face the intruder. This may not sound too terrifying to a curious naturalist, but at least some invertebrate predators are intimidated.

## ANGLEWINGS

Mourning Cloaks are not the only butterfly with peculiar food habits. Two species of *Polygonia* butterflies with grammatical names also favor sap, fruit, mud, and carrion over nectar. Commas (*Polygonia comma*) and Question Marks (*Polygonia interrogationis*) occur from the Gulf Coast to Canada and west to the Rockies.

As a group, anglewings are named for the unusual shape of their wings, which have an irregular, multiangled outline. Their genus name, *Polygonia,* means "many angles."

Anglewings lay eggs singly or in short stacks of as many as eight on the undersides of the leaves of host plants such as nettles, elms, and hackberries. Comma caterpillars pull down the edges of leaves and connect them with silk to form a tentlike refuge. Question Marks rarely make such nests.

The origin of the curious names of these two anglewings becomes clear upon careful examination. From above, Question Marks and Commas are handsome butterflies with burnt orange and black markings. Their underwings, however, are cryptically colored to mimic a dead leaf. When they perch with closed wings, they seem to disappear against a background of leaf litter or tree branches. On the underside of each hind wing of the Comma is a small, distinctive silver hook that resembles a comma. The Question Mark has a small silver dot just below the hook—a question mark. Any other name just wouldn't do.

## SPRING AZURES

Among the earliest of the spring butterflies to emerge are the tiny and delicate Spring Azures (*Celastrina argiolus*), which occur in all but the most northern reaches of North America. In the Midwest, they appear in March; in the Deep South, they fly in January. Spring Azures are just one species among a larger group of small blue butterflies known simply as the blues.

Unlike many butterflies, the Spring Azure uses a broad array of host plants, and this may account at least in part for its broad distribution. Curiously, the chosen host plants vary with the season. Early breeders lay their eggs on the leaves of dogwood and wild cherry; later-breeding females seem to prefer viburnum, sumac, and New Jersey tea. Other acceptable hosts include apple, oak, legumes, blueberry, and bittersweet.

Also unlike many butterflies, Azures lay their eggs on the buds and developing flowers of host plants. Azure caterpillars eat flowers and fruits and have the unusual ability to cultivate the protection of ants that live among them. A small gland on the caterpillar's abdomen secretes a sweet, clear liquid that ants love. The ants are so protective of their sugary food source that they attack any predator that threatens the Azure larva. This is no doubt another reason for the Azure's widespread distribution and success.

Two other blues found across North America are the Tailed Blue (*Everes comyntas*) and the Western Tailed Blue (*Everes amyntula*). The Tailed Blue occurs east of the Rockies and in parts of California, Oregon, New Mexico, and Arizona. The Western Tailed Blue is found west of the Great Plains and as far north as the Alaskan tundra. Larvae of both species eat the flowers and fruits of a variety of legumes, and both of these blues overwinter as mature caterpillars, unlike Azures, which overwinter as pupae.

## FRITILLARIES

I've never understood people so fanatical about the appearance of their lawn that they break out the weed killer when volunteer violets appear. These small purple flowers add color and character to any lawn, but more important, violets are the primary host plant for the thirty species of fritillary butterflies that inhabit North America. At least a few species of these medium to large orange and black butterflies occur virtually everywhere from Mexico to the high Arctic. But without violets, they'll never reproduce in your backyard.

Rather than lay their eggs directly on the host plant, as most butterflies do, some fritillaries lay their eggs rather haphazardly. They lay them near violets, but usually on twigs or stems of other plants or sometimes right on the ground. After hatching in late summer, the caterpillars hibernate, then find emerging violets in the spring.

## HARVESTERS

About fifty species of harvesters occur worldwide, but only one inhabits North America, and it is restricted to the eastern half of the United States. Every organism is unique in its own way, but among butterflies, Harvesters (*Feniseca tarquinius*) truly stand out. It's because of their diet.

The Harvester's proboscis is proportionately shorter in comparison with body length than that of any other butterfly. That's because it doesn't sip nectar from flowers. Rather, it sips "honeydew," which is just an entomologically correct name for aphid excrement. And though honeydew is its favorite food, it sometimes sips the urine and droppings of other creatures as well.

Despite the unusual nature of the adult Harvester's diet, the caterpillars' tastes are even stranger. Though most lepidopteran caterpillars eat leaves of specific host plants, harvester larvae are an exception. They are predators, the only carnivorous caterpillars in North America.

Female harvesters lay single eggs in the middle of colonies of woolly aphids. Upon hatching, the caterpillars spin a silk web to protect themselves from hungry ants. From their homespun shelter, they feast on woolly aphids, which typically occur on witch hazel, alder, beech, hawthorn, and currants. Because of this high-protein diet, Harvester caterpillars require only three molts before pupating in just a week to ten days. The pupa, which is marked by what resembles a monkey face, takes only about ten days to transform.

## SKIPPERS

To most nature-watchers, skippers are simply common, fast-flying butterflies. But taxonomically, they are not considered true butterflies. Among the biggest differences between skippers and the true butterflies, such as swallowtails and Monarchs, is that the tips of the skippers' antennae are distinctly bent—a minor detail to casual observers, but a major anatomical distinction to entomologists.

Skippers get their name from their powerful flight. Their bodies are thick and muscular compared with those of most butterflies, and it is that musculature that propels their strong flight.

Of the 263 species of skippers that occur in North America, the Silver-Spotted Skipper (*Epargyreus clarus*) is among the most widespread. Year in and year out, it outnumbers all other butterflies in my backyard. Blazing star (*Liatris* spp.) is a favorite nectar source. The silver spot on the underside of the hind wing is unique, so identification is relatively easy.

Skipper host plants include a wide variety of legumes. Eggs are laid singly on the tops of the leaves. Young caterpillars live inside folded leaves; older larvae secure leaves together with silk and live between them. They overwinter as pupae.

## SPHINX MOTHS

If it looks like a hummingbird, flies like a hummingbird, and feeds like a hummingbird, it should be a hummingbird, right? Not necessarily. If it's smaller than a hummer, it's probably a hummingbird moth.

Hummingbird moths are a type of sphinx moth. I often get calls about a strange, hummingbirdlike creature. Most report that it's fuzzy, looks like a bee, and has antennae and a long beak. Such detailed accounts, coupled with its habit of hovering above flowers while feeding, make identification easy.

About one hundred species of sphinx moths inhabit North America. The first one I ever saw in flight was on the shore of Lake Powell in northern Arizona. And at first, like everyone else, I was puzzled. I thought I had spotted one of the many hummingbirds that inhabit the western United States. But a quick survey of my field guides introduced me to these curious moths.

Most sphinx moths are active at dusk and after dark, when they sip the nectar of tubular flowers that remain open at night. In return for the meal, they pollinate the flowers. The "beak" is actually the proboscis, a long, flexible tube that stays coiled under the head when the moth is not feeding.

Several species are most likely to be seen. One is small with a body that's only about an inch long. Others are larger, but still smaller than hummers.

Clearwing Hummingbird Moths (*Hemaris thysbe*) are among the smallest of these fascinating insects. I usually see the first ones in early June at midday, drinking nectar from the blooms on my lilac bushes. If I approach slowly, I sometimes can observe one carefully for several minutes. Its long proboscis uncoils as it approaches each flower, and its transparent wings are obvious.

The White-Lined Sphinx (*Hyles lineata*) has a long, white line extending the length of the front wing and a rosy-colored stripe across the rear wing. The heavy, brown body tapers to a point at each end and has a series of dark bands across the abdomen.

The other common local species is best known by the name of its caterpillar and is probably more familiar to readers who garden. Tomato Hornworms, those fat, green, fleshy caterpillars that eat your tomatoes and their leaves, eventually transform into Five-Spotted Hawkmoths (*Manduca quinquemaculata*). The adults are large, gray moths with a wingspan of about 4 inches. A series of five or six bright orange spots on each side of the abdomen helps identify them.

The larval hornworm got its name from the soft, spinelike "horn" that projects upward from the rear end of the body. Though the spine looks like a stinger, it's quite harmless. When alarmed, hornworms erect themselves in a stiff, sphinxlike pose, hence the general name of this group of moths.

A Tomato Hornworm has eight V-shaped, white marks on its sides, and its horn is black. Other species are marked differently and may have different colored horns.

If you find hornworms covered with tiny white capsules, be relieved, not alarmed. These white objects are pupal cases of tiny wasps that parasitize hornworms and control their numbers. They are harmless to people. By the time these pupae hatch, the hornworm will be dead. The larval wasps consumed the hornworm from the inside before emerging to pupate.

The life cycle of sphinx moths is simple and includes a complete metamorphosis. Early in the summer, females lay up to three hundred eggs on the undersides of leaves of tomatoes and other host plants, such as peppers, potatoes, petunias, and geraniums. In about a week, the caterpillars hatch. They feed furiously for the next four to six weeks and molt five times before burrowing underground to pupate for the winter. The following June, adults emerge and repeat the life cycle.

## LUNA MOTHS

A few years ago, I spent two weeks on an island just off the coast of Maine. It was a great time, full of outdoor adventures and new discoveries. One of the highlights was a freshly emerged Luna Moth on the cabin screen door almost every morning. Here in West Virginia, I'm lucky if I see more than a handful each year.

Luna moths (*Actias luna*) are spectacular members of the giant silkworm family. Their large size and lime green color make them easy to recognize, though the distinctive color fades quickly when exposed to sunlight. Their wingspan can measure up to 4 inches, and their hind wings extend into long, sweeping tails. Though Lunas can be accurately described as "swallow-tailed," they are unrelated to swallowtail butterflies.

The color on the edges of the wings varies seasonally. Lunas from spring broods have pink, reddish brown, or purplish margins. The wings of Lunas that emerge in midsummer are trimmed in yellow. And each wing carries a transparent spot accented with a dark border.

Moths dominate the lepidopteran realm. Of more than 140,000 species of butterflies and moths found worldwide, only about 10 percent are butterflies. But butterflies are more colorful, active during the day, and desirable. Moths tend to be drab and nocturnal, and many are pests. Consequently, it's no surprise we favor butterflies.

But if you survey the area beneath an outdoor light each morning, you may find dozens of memorable moths, many of which are large and strikingly marked. The Luna Moth is my favorite. Its color is sublime, and its size is magnificent. The Luna is the queen of the night, and when we're lucky, she lingers in the dooryard at dawn. Graceful and elegant may seem like odd adjectives to describe a moth, but the Luna Moth is the first lady of the insect world, and she can hold her own even in comparison with Monarchs and swallowtails.

Another feature you'll notice on any Luna that graces the back porch are its large, feathery antennae. These are chemical receptors, capable of detecting the scent of another Luna. This is how males and females, which are active only at night, find each other to mate. Female silkworm moths can dispense just a billionth of a gram of pheromone per hour and attract males from as far as a mile away. Moth olfaction makes mammalian noses seem downright primitive.

After mating, the female Luna lays clusters of eggs on the twigs of trees whose leaves its caterpillars devour—hickory, walnut, cherry, beech, pecan, persimmon, sweet gum, maple, and willow. According to University of Illinois entomologist May Berenbaum, author of *Ninety-nine Gnats, Nits and Nibblers* and *Ninety-nine More Maggots, Mites and Munchers,* a newly hatched Luna caterpillar weighs just $^1/_{20}$ gram and grows to more than 200 grams when it's ready to spin a cocoon in six to eight weeks. That's a weight gain of more than four thousand times its hatching weight!

Mature Luna caterpillars can sometimes be found by searching leaves above piles of frass, fecal pellets that accumulate beneath the hungry, ever-eating larvae. The thick, green, fleshy body can approach 3 inches in length. A yellow stripe runs along both sides of the abdomen, and many small, orange knobs called tubercles decorate the entire body.

In late summer, the Luna caterpillar pulls together several leaves with silk and weaves a cocoon. After the autumnal leaf fall, the cocoon lies hidden amid the leaf litter on the forest floor until spring. In late April or May, metamorphosis is complete, and a new Luna Moth emerges. Males then wait for just the faintest whiff of a female's irresistible scent.

## EASTERN TENT CATERPILLARS

There is no more ordinary creature than the Eastern Tent Caterpillar (*Malacosma americanum*). Each spring their distinctive silky tents can be found in woods, old fields, and along country roads. Yet their life history is as extraordinary and mysterious as that of any of their lepidopteran kin.

Tent caterpillars spend most of their lives inside an egg. Adult moths live just a few days. The form we know best, the caterpillar, is the most conspicuous.

In late June or early July, a small, brown moth struggles free from a cocoon fastened to the inside of a slab of loose bark on an old, dying tree. Blood courses through its unfurling wings; within a few hours the 1$^1/_2$-inch moth is on the wing. It wanders purposefully, led by olfactory cues, in search of a mate. Within forty-eight hours, the female is bred. Now she searches for an apple, cherry, or other fruit tree. She deposits a cluster of two hundred to three hundred eggs around a small twig. Their responsibilities satisfied, adult males and females die just a few days after emerging from the cocoon.

The moth's destiny now lies inside the egg case that hardens on the twig. Through the blistering heat of summer and the frigid cold of winter, the eggs lie dormant, shielded from the elements only by the thin protective membrane of the egg case. Thanks to a natural antifreeze called glycerol, which makes up 35 percent of the egg's weight by January, the fluids in the embryo remain unfrozen.

Inside the egg, a biological clock ticks, marking off the months until spring's longer days trigger the clock's alarm. The eggs hatch in April, and tiny, hungry caterpillars emerge. They migrate downward toward a centrally located crotch in the tree and begin spinning and weaving the familiar tent. The caterpillars work in shifts to build a shelter that consists of many horizontal layers, not unlike a dish of lasagna or baklava. The space between each layer is just large enough to accommodate a group of caterpillars.

When not resting or building the tent, tent caterpillars march upward along the tree's smallest branches in search of fresh, tender leaves. They eat voraciously and grow rapidly. To ensure that they can find their way back to the tent, tent caterpillars leave behind a trail of silk. The combined efforts of the colony yield an extensive network of silky trails that always lead home. If Hansel and Gretel had been so skilled, the Brothers Grimm would have had one less fairy tale to tell.

Insect growth is limited by an elastic exoskeleton that can stretch only so far. It then splits, and the old exoskeleton is shed. Tent caterpillars molt six times from April through June. Each time, hormones control the process to ensure that a new, larger caterpillar, rather than a premature moth, results.

After the final molt, the concentration of juvenile hormones ebbs so that when the mature caterpillar attains a certain critical weight, the next transformation is far more dramatic. At this critical size, other hormones kick in. Caterpillars lose their appetite and wander in search of a place to pupate. This is when we see them crossing roads, trails, and lawns.

Under a log, rock, or slab of bark, the tent caterpillar undergoes its final and most miraculous transformation. First it weaves itself a silky cocoon, leaving a weak spot from which its final incarnation can emerge. Over the course of the next three weeks, the caterpillar physiologically and biochemically transforms itself from hairy caterpillar to scale-covered moth.

The single purpose of the adult moth is to reproduce. That done, the short-lived moth dies, and a new generation of eggs awaits the following spring. It's an extraordinary story for such an ordinary creature.

## FALL WEBWORMS
Phenology is the study of predictable biological events influenced primarily by climate. Migratory birds head south in the fall and return north in

the spring. The deer rut occurs in late October and November. Woodchucks and chipmunks hibernate in the winter. Forests green up in April. And as summer winds down, brilliantly colored goldfinches frequent roadside patches of thistle, nighthawks sweep across the evening sky, and Fall Webworms begin to litter trees in backyards and woodlands.

As I gaze across the yard into the woods, my eyes are drawn to what seem like small, wispy clouds. They are nests of the Fall Webworm, the caterpillar of a small, white moth that rarely attracts attention. In fact, the moth that arises from a Fall Webworm is so nondescript it doesn't even warrant a name. A Field Guide to Moths: Eastern North America simply calls it the Fall Webworm Moth.

Webworms are common and native to much of the United States. I see them every year. Many trees, from apples and cherries to persimmons and walnuts, can be victimized. Mild winters and cool, wet summers favor webworms, so the following year can bring a severe outbreak.

Unlike Eastern Tent Caterpillars, which appear in the spring and weave their webs in the crotches of trees, Fall Webworms appear in late summer and build their webs on the outer tips of branches. Tent caterpillars eat young, vigorous leaves, whereas webworms eat leaves that have already done most of their work for the tree. As summer winds down, plant growth slows, and leaf loss is much less serious than when it occurs in spring or early summer. Fall Webworms are never a pretty sight, but neither are they particularly worrisome.

Web building begins when the first eggs hatch, usually in early July. Females lay as many as four hundred eggs on the leaves of favorite foods, and when the caterpillars hatch, they begin building the web. Over the course of four to six weeks, the caterpillars molt six times and grow to about 1½ inches in length. Then they leave the nest, drop to the ground, and find a place to pupate under a rock or a slab of bark. There they spend the fall and winter. In late May or June, adults emerge from their cocoons, mate, and die. The adult moth stage lives only a few weeks.

To protect themselves from hungry birds and other predators, webworms stay inside their webs and eat the leaves enveloped by the silky shelter. This is another difference between webworms and tent caterpillars—tent caterpillars leave their tents to eat fresh leafy growth.

If it sometimes seems that evidence of Fall Webworms appears overnight, that may be the case. Webworms, which are recognized by long white or pale yellow hairs on each body segment, work all night long, and after the colony grows to a certain size, the web grows quickly. A large nest may be 3 or 4 feet long and encase several branches.

For those who wish to combat webworms, there are several options. A popular, though dangerous, treatment is to burn the nests. I discourage this choice because it can damage trees, cause brush or forest fires, and kill people. Instead, open webs with a stick to give predators such as cuckoos, orioles, and vireos access to the caterpillars, or apply BT (*Bacillus thuringiensis*) according to label instructions. If you have just a few webs, you might consider simply pruning the tented branches and destroying them. Because webworms usually don't cause permanent damage, I recommend a laissez-faire approach.

## GYPSY MOTHS

In the midst of a heavy Gypsy Moth outbreak, forests lose their leaves, individual trees die, and the rain of droppings, or frass, from caterpillars munching leaves in the treetops can be seen, heard, and felt. It's not a pretty picture.

In fact, the U.S. Forest Service reports that Gypsy Moths have been the primary defoliator of northeastern deciduous trees, especially oaks, since 1869. That's when a French biologist imported some to Massachusetts in an attempt to develop a hardy, silk-producing caterpillar.

Gypsy Moths turned out to be quite hardy, but otherwise the experiment failed. The western front of the Gypsy Moth invasion advances every year.

The Gypsy Moth life cycle begins when flightless females lay egg masses in mid to late summer. The buff-colored, fuzzy egg cases, which measure 1 to 1$\frac{1}{2}$ inches long and $\frac{1}{2}$ inch wide, contain one hundred to five hundred eggs. Look for them on tree trunks, rocks, buildings, woodpiles, birdhouses, and even vehicles.

After overwintering in the egg case stage, a new generation hatches in late April or early May. Newly hatched caterpillars are tiny and inconspicuous.

They are attracted to light, so they climb high into the treetops. From there, they disperse over wide areas by a process entomologists call ballooning. The caterpillars release long, silky threads and are blown from the treetops by the wind. In mountainous areas, young caterpillars may disperse as many as 4 miles from the hatch site. This is one way outbreaks spread from year to year.

In June, caterpillars grow rapidly and molt several times. The final and largest instar, or caterpillar stage, does most of the visible damage to trees. Favorite foods include leaves of oak, apple, pine, hemlock, blue spruce, and willow. This most voracious instar is 2 inches long, hairy, and recognized by the five pairs of blue spots and six pairs of red spots that line its back.

In late June or early July, caterpillars transform into the dormant pupal stage, which lasts ten to seventeen days. Then adult moths emerge.

Females release powerful pheromones to attract males. After mating and laying new egg cases, the adults die, and the population's future rests again with the army of egg cases littering the woods.

Unfortunately, even though we understand the Gypsy Moth life cycle, we can't eradicate these pests. But Gypsy Moth damage is easier to accept if we understand the biological value of dead trees. Trees that die become snags that shelter woodpeckers and other cavity-nesting wildlife. The extra sunlight that reaches the forest floor stimulates the growth of ground cover and understory vegetation. That's good for deer and dozens of songbirds. And the nutrients locked away in the wood enrich the soil when the snags eventually fall and rot.

Yes, Gypsy Moths change the appearance of the woods. But change is what nature's all about.

If you want to protect a favorite shade tree or an entire stand of timber, there are several possible controls available to landowners. Which is best is subject to debate and controversy.

Environmentalists favor a hands-off approach unless you're growing timber for profit or you want to protect a few valuable shade trees. In those cases, spraying BT (Bacillus thuringiensis), a natural bacterium that kills Gypsy Moth caterpillars, might be justified, though it can kill nontarget lepidopteran larvae as well.

A less destructive option is wrapping valued trees with burlap bands at chest height. During the day, caterpillars hide under the burlap flaps, where they are easily collected and destroyed.

Another manual control is collecting and destroying egg cases during the fall and winter. Use a spoon or putty knife to gather the egg cases, because the fibers that protect the eggs irritate human skin. And be sure to destroy them, as egg cases left on the ground can survive the winter.

Prevention is also possible. Keep backyard trees healthy by mulching, watering, and fertilizing wisely. Avoid disturbing or compacting the soil around valuable trees. And plant species such as ash, dogwood, grape, and holly, which Gypsy Moths eat only when favorite foods are unavailable.

## WOOLLY BEARS

Frost on the pumpkin, honking geese overhead, hungry juncos in the yard, and a symphony of color in the woods—fall has arrived, and already you can feel winter closing in. An equally reliable sign of fall is the intermittent parade of Woolly Bears that marches along and across country roads. Some days you may see dozens, on a trip to some secret hideaway that even they don't understand. They are driven by the changing photoperiod—shorter days—which in turn directs their hormones and instincts, telling them to search for winter shelter. They may find it under a tuft of grass, beneath a pile of leaves, in a hollow log, or under a rock. There they curl into a ball and while away the winter in a dormant state.

Come spring, Woolly Bears leave their shelter and, driven now by hunger, gorge on dandelions, pig's ears, and grasses. Then they spin a silky cocoon and begin the mysterious transformation from caterpillar into moth. In late May, adult Isabella Moths (*Pyrrharctica isabella*) emerge. Unlike their well-known larval stage, Isabella Moths are nondescript and unknown to most naturalists. They mature quickly and spawn a summer brood of Woolly Bears. It is the subsequent summer moths that lay the eggs that become the caterpillars we see each fall. Hence, Isabella Moths breed twice a year.

Fascinating as the natural history of Woolly Bears may be, it is their alleged weather forecasting skill that captures the imagination. Woolly Bears are easily recognized. They are about 2 inches long, hairy, and black with a rust-colored band encircling the midsection. It is the rusty band that tells the tale. Folklore has it that the width of the rusty band can predict the severity of the coming winter. The narrower the rusty band, and hence the blacker the Woolly Bear, the more severe the coming winter will be.

Actually, Woolly Bears do not predict the weather; they react to it. It is their physiological and anatomical reactions that probably gave rise to this bit of folklore.

A Woolly Bear's rusty band widens with age. Each time the caterpillar molts, it emerges with a wider rusty band. Unseasonably cold fall mornings send younger individuals scurrying in search of winter shelter. So off they go, through woods and fields, across roads and highways. Older, rustier caterpillars, meanwhile, have already retired for the winter. That's why we see so many mostly black Woolly Bears on chilly mornings. It is not unreasonable that someone somewhere would make a connection between Woolly Bears with narrow rusty bands and a hard winter.

In truth, however, what we see reflects current conditions, not a prediction of the future. Heck, professional meteorologists have a hard time nailing a five-day forecast; why should we expect better from a lowly caterpillar?

The Woolly Bear gets its name from the long hairs that cover its body, but the covering is far from woolly. The hairs are short, stiff, and bristly. They help protect the fleshy caterpillar from predators. Many predators avoid bristly, irritating food items. When a Woolly Bear is disturbed, it simply curls up into a ball—a seemingly lifeless fuzzball.

Few charades are foolproof, however. Skunks roll Woolly Bears around on the ground until the hairs fall off. And birds such as orioles, tanagers, and cuckoos whack hairy caterpillars against branches to remove the bristly hairs.

If you find a Woolly Bear, examine it carefully. If its rusty band is narrow, the caterpillar is relatively young. And the coming winter? Your guess is as good as the Woolly Bear's.

# CHAPTER 3

# Species Accounts

For years, whenever I discovered a new butterfly, I was frustrated when I tried to learn more about it. What did its caterpillars eat? How did it get through the winter? What were its favorite nectar sources? Some field guides contained some of this information, but it was difficult to track this basic natural history information down quickly. Today there are large reference books that answer most of these questions, but even curious naturalists often resist spending $50 or more for reference books they'll seldom use.

This chapter provides the basic life history data for some common species of butterflies and moths, arranged by family. As this book is not a field identification guide, the descriptions are brief and mention only the most obvious identifying characters. I suggest you also keep a field guide handy for times when questions about identification arise.

## SWALLOWTAILS (Family Papilionidae)

### Pipevine Swallowtail (*Battus philenor*)

**Eggs:** Reddish brown; laid in clusters of up to twenty on underside of host plant leaves.

**Caterpillar:** Dark purplish black with red and black fleshy filaments on each segment; filaments on first segment quite long. Poisonous to predators due to toxins in host plant. Young caterpillars feed in groups (being toxic allows them to be conspicuous).

**Adult:** 2.75- to 4.5-inch wingspan. From above, black with iridescent blue-green rear wing; underside of hind wing has U-shaped row of seven orange warning spots on iridescent field of blue.

**Habitat:** Deciduous forests, often along streams.

**Range:** East of a line from Wisconsin to central California.

**Comments:** Males patrol. Two to four broods per year. Like the Monarch, has a tough, leathery abdomen that's difficult for predators to bite.

**Winter strategy:** Hibernates as pupa.

**Caterpillar host plants:** Pipevine, Dutchman's pipe, snakeroot.

**Adult food sources:** Thistle, milkweed, honeysuckle, azalea, lilac, butterfly bush.


## Zebra Swallowtail (*Eurytides marcellus*)

**Eggs:** Pale green; laid singly on pawpaw leaves.

**Caterpillar:** Pale green and fleshy, with fine black and yellow lines across each segment.

**Adult:** 2.25- to 3.5-inch wingspan. Like its namesake, marked by bold black and off-white stripes. Two blue spots and one red spot on edge of upper surface of hind wing. Summer brood is larger and has longer "tails."

**Habitat:** Moist, deciduous forests, often along streams and rivers. Ventures into fields for nectar plants.

**Range:** Eastern half of U.S. from southern Wisconsin and Michigan to New York and New England.

**Comments:** Males patrol near pawpaw. Two broods per year. Batlike flight.

**Winter strategy:** Hibernates as pupa.

**Caterpillar host plants:** Pawpaw.

**Adult food sources:** Milkweed, redbud, blackberry, dogbane, verbena, puddles on moist soils. The Zebra Swallowtail has a relatively short proboscis, so it cannot use long tubular flowers.


## Black Swallowtail (*Papilio polyxenes*)

**Eggs:** Cream-colored; laid singly on host plant leaves and flowers. Female lays thirty to fifty eggs per day for up to ten days

**Caterpillar:** Large, fleshy, yellow-green with black bands between segments; yellow spots on the black bands.

**Adult:** 2.5- to 3.5-inch wingspan. Black with two rows of yellow spots along wing margins.

**Habitat:** Fields, roadsides, meadows, woodlands.

**Range:** East of Rocky Mountains in U.S. and southern Canada.

**Comments:** One (north) to many (south) broods per year. Males perch and patrol.

**Winter strategy:** Pupa hibernates.

**Caterpillar host plants:** Parsley, dill, celery, Queen Anne's lace, and other members of carrot family.

**Adult food sources:** Milkweed, clover, thistle, phlox, butterfly bush.

## Giant Swallowtail (*Papilio cresphontes*)

**Eggs:** Yellow, green, or orange; laid singly on host plant leaves and twigs.

**Caterpillar:** Mimics bird droppings. Considered a pest of citrus trees, so plant them to attract this species.

**Adult:** 3.5- to 5.5-inch wingspan; one of largest butterflies in North America. Black with large yellow stripe across each front wing and yellow spots on margins of hind wing.

**Habitat:** Orchards, parks, open fields.

**Range:** East of the Rockies and Southern California, Arizona, and New Mexico.

**Comments:** Two (north) to many (south) broods per year. Male patrols.

**Winter strategy:** Pupa hibernates.

**Caterpillar host plants:** Orange, other citrus trees, prickly ash.

**Adult food sources:** Honeysuckle, lantana, azalea, mud, and fresh manure (for nutrients and minerals).

## Spicebush Swallowtail (*Papilio troilus*)

**Eggs:** Pale green; laid singly on underside of host plant leaves.

**Caterpillar:** Large, green, and fleshy with large eyespots. Older caterpillars roll food plant leaves and live inside. Turns bright yellow before pupating.

**Adult:** 3- to 5-inch wingspan. Dark with iridescent green or blue patches on hind wings and white spots on wing margins. Mimics poisonous Pipevine Swallowtail.

**Habitat:** Open woodlands and forest edges.

**Range:** East of Rockies.

**Comments:** Males patrol. Several broods per year; first appear in April.

**Winter strategy:** Overwinters as pupa on stems near ground.

**Caterpillar host plants:** Spicebush, sassafras, bay.
**Adult food sources:** Milkweed, thistle, ironweed, joe-pye weed, honey-suckle, mud (for minerals).

### Eastern Tiger Swallowtail (*Papilio glaucus*)

**Eggs:** Green; laid singly on host plant leaves.
**Caterpillar:** Young caterpillar resembles brown and white bird droppings; older larva turns green and mimics small snake with orange eyespots.
**Adult:** 4- to 5-inch wingspan. Bright yellow with black markings. Replaced in West by similar Western Tiger Swallowtail and in Canada by Canadian Tiger Swallowtail.
**Habitat:** Deciduous woods, forest openings, and edges.
**Range:** East of central Great Plains
**Comments:** Cryptically colored brown chrysalis suspended from twig. Males patrol. One brood in north, two in south. Females dimorphic—some yellow like males, some black; black form most common in south, where it mimics foul-tasting Pipevine Swallowtail.
**Winter strategy:** Hibernates as pupa in leaf litter.
**Caterpillar host plants:** Many deciduous trees, including lilac, willow, tulip poplar, cherry, birch.
**Adult food sources:** Joe-pye weed, bee balm, butterfly bush, lilies, clover, azalea; carrion; large aggregations of males often "puddle" along streams or at pools of fresh urine in search of sodium

## SULPHURS AND WHITES (Family Pieridae)

### Orange Sulphur (*Colias eurytheme*)

**Eggs:** Pale, turning reddish after several days; laid singly on host plant leaves. Female lays about seven hundred eggs.
**Caterpillar:** Small, green, fleshy with white or multicolored lateral line.
**Adult:** 1.25- to 2.25-inch wingspan. Common and widespread over most of North America. Yellow-orange wings with black border; females often white with black wing borders.
**Habitat:** Open fields, pastures, hayfields, meadows.
**Range:** U.S. and southern half of Canada.

**Comments:** Three (north) to five (south) broods per year. Males patrol.

**Winter strategy:** Hibernates as third or forth instar larva.

**Caterpillar host plants:** Alfalfa, clover, vetch, lupine.

**Adult food sources:** Dandelion, teasel, ironweed, thistle, goldenrod, mud.

## Common Sulphur (*Colias philodice*)

**Eggs:** Cream-colored, turning red after a day or two; laid singly on host plant leaves.

**Caterpillar:** Small, green, and fleshy, similar to Orange Sulphur; green head.

**Adult:** 1- to 2-inch wingspan. Occurs over most of North America. Similar to but less orange than *C. eurytheme,* with which it hybridizes. Females dimorphic, about one-third being white.

**Habitat:** Open fields, pastures, meadows.

**Range:** U.S. and western Canada, north to most of Alaska.

**Comments:** Three (north) to five (south) broods per year. Most adults live two to three days. Can be a pest in alfalfa fields. Males patrol.

**Winter strategy:** Hibernates as third or fourth instar larva.

**Caterpillar host plants:** Clover and other legumes.

**Adult food sources:** Dandelion, clover, goldenrod, ironweed, aster, joe-pye weed.

## Cabbage White (*Pieris rapae*)

**Eggs:** White or pale yellow; laid singly on host plant leaves.

**Caterpillar:** Small, fleshy, bluish green with row of yellow dashes along sides; green head.

**Adult:** 1.25- to 1.75-inch wingspan. White with black tips on front wings.

**Habitat:** Open fields, pastures, yards, gardens.

**Range:** U.S. and southern Canada.

**Comments:** Introduced from Europe to Canada in 1860. Can be a garden pest. Distasteful to predators due to mustard oils larvae ingest. Males patrol. One to many broods per year. Twenty-one species of whites occur in North America.

**Winter strategy:** Overwinters as pupa.

**Caterpillar host plants:** Cabbage, broccoli, cauliflower, mustard.

**Adult food sources:** Dandelion, mustard, mint, aster.

## BRUSH-FOOTED BUTTERFLIES (Family Nymphalidae)

### Monarch (*Danaus plexippus*)

**Eggs:** Pale green; laid singly under milkweed leaves or on stems and flowers.

**Caterpillar:** Fleshy body encircled with alternating bands of white, black, and yellow. Two black, antennalike structures at each end.

**Adult:** 3.5- to 4-inch wingspan. Burnt orange wings with black veins and margins. Chrysalis shiny lime green and flecked with spots of gold.

**Habitat:** Open fields, roadsides, rights-of-way.

**Range:** U.S. and southern Canada.

**Comments:** Caterpillar eats milkweed and incorporates plant's toxins into its tissues, making both caterpillars and adults inedible. Just prior to emergence, chrysalis becomes clear, making adult visible. Males have scent gland, which appears as a large, black spot on vein near center of hind wings; pheromone from this gland excites females during courtship. Male flies joined with female on "postnuptial" flight.

**Winter strategy:** Adults migrate; summer's last brood migrates south to mountains in central Mexico or Southern California (western populations).

**Caterpillar host plants:** Milkweed.

**Adult food sources:** Milkweed, clover, zinnia, daisy, aster.

### Wood Nymph (*Cercyonis pegala*)

**Eggs:** Pale yellow, turning tan in about five days; laid carelessly on or near grasses. Female lays as many as three hundred eggs.

**Caterpillar:** Four yellow longitudinal stripes mark the yellow-green body, covered with short hairs. Final abdominal segment appears to be a forked "tail."

**Adult:** 2-inch wingspan. Dull brown with two eyespots on front wings. Curious "hopping" flight. Common, widespread member of a group of butterflies called satyrs.

**Habitat:** Woodlands, forest edges, open fields.

**Range:** Southern Canada and U.S., except southwest from Texas to California.

**Comments:** One brood per year. Males patrol.

**Winter strategy:** First instar larva hibernates.

**Caterpillar host plants:** Various grasses.

**Adult food sources:** Sap flows, rotting fruit, dung, and nectar from most flowers.


## Viceroy (*Limenitis archippus*)

**Eggs:** Pale green; laid singly on upper tips of young host plant leaves.

**Caterpillar:** Brown or green with white saddle; resembles bird dropping; chrysalis also mimics bird dropping.

**Adult:** 2.5- to 3-inch wingspan. Adults mimic Monarchs to avoid predators, though they usually are not toxic (some Florida populations have been found to be toxic due to eating toxic plant material). Black line running through midsection of hind wings distinguishes Viceroys from Monarchs.

**Habitat:** Wet meadows, streamsides, ponds.

**Range:** Eastern three-quarters of U.S. and Canada.

**Comments:** Two to three broods per year. Flap, flap, glide flight pattern.

**Winter strategy:** Winters as third instar caterpillar in rolled-up leaves.

**Caterpillar host plants:** Willow, poplar, aspen, cottonwood, apple, cherry, plum.

**Adult food sources:** Dung, carrion, rotting fruit, mud, sap, milkweed, aster, clover, zinnia, joe-pye weed, daisy, thistle, teasel.


## Red-Spotted Purple and White Admiral (*Limenitis arthemis*)

**Eggs:** Gray-green; laid singly on top of host plant leaves.

**Caterpillar:** Brown and white; mimics bird dropping; chrysalis also resembles bird dropping.

**Adult:** 2.5- to 3.5-inch wingspan. Common butterfly occurring in two distinct forms: Red-Spotted Purple (south) has black and white spots on margin of front wings and iridescent blue-green areas on outer portion of hind wings; White Admiral (north) has connecting broad, white bands on front and hind wings; these two forms freely hybridize where populations overlap.

**Habitat:** Woodlands and forest edges.

**Range:** Eastern half of U.S. and most of Canada.

**Comments:** Two to three broods per year. Red-Spotted Purple mimics distasteful Pipevine Swallowtail.

**Winter strategy:** Overwinters as third instar larva encased in leaf rolled up into "tube hibernaculum."

**Caterpillar host plants:** Cherry, aspen, apple, oak, willow, hawthorn.

**Adult food sources:** Sap flows, carrion, dung, rotting fruit, decaying wood, and nectar from most flowers.


## Buckeye (*Junonia coenia*)

**Eggs:** Dark green; laid singly.

**Caterpillar:** Spiny black body with two rows of orange spots along back and two rows of cream spots on each side; branched spines on back have blue bases; branched spines on sides have orange bases. Eats leaves, buds, and fruits.

**Adult:** 1.5- to 2.5-inch wingspan. Beautiful brown butterfly with orange bars and two conspicuous eyespots on each wing.

**Habitat:** Open fields, roadsides, dunes, rights-of-way.

**Range:** U.S. and southern Canada; absent from northern Rockies and Washington.

**Comments:** Two to three broods per year. Males perch. Adults live about ten days.

**Winter strategy:** Larvae and some adults hibernate in south; recolonize northern areas via spring-summer migrations.

**Caterpillar host plants:** Plantain, snapdragon, verbena.

**Adult food sources:** Clover, Queen Anne's lace, sunflower, milkweed, ironweed, aster, mud.


## Red Admiral (*Vanessa atalanta*)

**Eggs:** Pale green; laid singly on top surface of host plant leaves.

**Caterpillar:** Variable; yellow, gray, red, or black body with many branching spines.

**Adult:** 2-inch wingspan. Dark wings with orange bands crossing front wings and on outer margin of hind wings; white spots on top of front wings; reddish orange bars on upper surface of all four wings.

**Habitat:** Forest edges and clearings, roadsides, riparian zones.

**Range:** U.S. and southern half of Canada.

Black Swallowtail
*(Papilio polyxenes)*

Eastern Tiger Swallowtail
*(Papilio glaucus)*

Spicebush Swallowtail
*(Papilio troilus)*

Cabbage White
*(Pieris rapae)*

Common Sulphur
*(Colias philodice)*

Orange Sulphur
*(Colias eurytheme)*

Spring Azure
(*Celastrina ladon*)

Hummingbird
Clearwing Moth
(*Hemaris thysbe*)

Pipevine Swallowtail
(*Battus philenor*)

Gray Hairstreak
(*Strymon melinus*)

American Snout
(*Libytheana carinenta*)

Great Spangled Fritillary
(*Speyeria cybele*)

Viceroy
(*Limenitis archippus*)

Pearl Crescent
(*Phyciodes tharos*)

Question Mark
(*Polygonia interrogationis*)

Painted Lady
*(Vanessa cardui)*

Red Admiral
*(Vanessa atalanta)*

Buckeye
*(Junonia coenia)*

Red-spotted Purple
(*Limenitis arthemis*)

Luna Moth
(*Actias luna*)

Monarch
(*Danaus plexippus*)

Silver-spotted Skipper
(*Epargyreus clarus*)

Polyphemus Moth
(*Antheraea polyphemus*)

ABOVE: Hummingbird/butterfly
garden, Marion County, Illinois

LEFT: Garden with salvias,
asters, petunias, artemisias,
and baby's breath

**Comments:** At least two broods per year. Males perch. Rapid, erratic flight. Aggressive, often chase other butterflies. Occur worldwide in Europe, Asia, North Africa, Hawaii, and New Zealand.

**Winter strategy:** Adults hibernate in south, then recolonize northern range with annual northward migration.

**Caterpillar host plants:** Nettle, false nettle, hops.

**Adult food sources:** Sap flows, rotting fruit, milkweed, cosmos.


## Painted Lady (*Vanessa cardui*)

**Eggs:** Pale green; laid singly on top side of host plant leaves.

**Caterpillar:** Spiny, dark with yellow lines along sides.

**Adult:** 1.5- to 2.5-inch wingspan. Similar to American Lady. Underside of hind wing has four small, black eyespots outlined in blue.

**Habitat:** Open fields, marshes, gardens, deserts.

**Range:** U.S. and southern two-thirds of Canada.

**Comments:** One to three broods per year; many broods in the south. Males perch. Occurs worldwide. This is the species biological supply houses sell to schools to demonstrate insects' life cycles.

**Winter strategy:** Adults hibernate in south; recolonize north with northward migration; sometimes move north from Mexico in tremendous numbers.

**Caterpillar host plants:** Thistle, aster, hollyhock, other mallows.

**Adult food sources:** Thistle, ironweed, aster, clover, zinnia, marigold, joe-pye weed.


## American Painted Lady (*Vanessa virginiensis*)

**Eggs:** Pale green; laid singly on upper leaf surface.

**Caterpillar:** Black with narrow yellow bands.

**Adult:** 1.5- to 2.5-inch wingspan. Black, orange, and white, similar to Painted Lady; underside of hind wings have two large eyespots. Similar Western Painted Lady (*V. carye*) replaces American Lady in West.

**Habitat:** Open fields, rights-of-way, roadsides, streambanks.

**Range:** U.S. and southern Canada.

**Comments:** Two broods per year. Many broods in south. Males perch.

**Winter strategy:** Adults hibernate, then migrate to recolonize northern range each year.

**Caterpillar host plants:** Pussytoes, everlasting, nettle, thistle, lupine, sunflowers.

**Adult food sources:** Daisy, burdock, mallow, yarrow, zinnia, milkweed, clover, dandelion, goldenrod.


## Question Mark (Polygonia interrogationis)

**Eggs:** Pale green; laid singly or stacked in piles of up to eight, like a stack of hotcakes.

**Caterpillar:** Black with many white spots; orange stripe along sides; yellow stripe on top; covered with orange and yellow branching spines. Brown chrysalis mimics dead leaf.

**Adult:** 2.5-inch wingspan. Adult burnt orange with ragged wing margins and "tails" on hind wings. Silver "question mark" on underside of hind wings. Mimics dead leaf with wings closed. Two seasonal forms; winter form is more orange.

**Habitat:** Woodlands, swamps, forest edges.

**Range:** East of Rockies in U.S. and southern Canada.

**Comments:** Two broods per year. Males perch.

**Winter strategy:** Hibernates as adult under loose slabs of bark or in hollow trees; one of the few species that might use a butterfly "hibernation" box.

**Caterpillar host plants:** Elm, hackberry, hops, nettle, false nettle.

**Adult food sources:** Sap flows, animal dung, rotting fruit.


## Eastern Comma or Comma Anglewing (Polygonia comma)

**Eggs:** Pale green; laid singly or stacked in piles of up to eight on underside of host plant leaves.

**Caterpillar:** Variable: pale yellow, reddish brown, or black; may or may not have colorful markings; all covered with spines.

**Adult:** 1.75- to 2-inch wingspan. Drab, cryptic coloration. Distinctive silver "comma" on underside of hind wings. Mimics dead leaf with wings closed.

**Habitat:** Moist woodlands.

**Range:** East of Rockies in U.S. and southern Canada; in Southwest only to eastern Oklahoma and Texas.

**Comments:** Two broods per year. Males perch. Aggressive, will chase other butterflies. Adults hide in hollow trees on hot summer days.

**Winter strategy:** Hibernates as adult under loose slabs of bark or in hollow trees; another of the few species that might use a butterfly "hibernation" box.

**Caterpillar host plants:** Nettle, false nettle, hops, elm.

**Adult food sources:** Dung, fruits, puddles, carrion.

## Milbert's Tortoise Shell (Nymphalis milberti)

**Eggs:** Pale green; laid in clusters of hundreds on underside of host plant leaves.

**Caterpillar:** Black with orange and white dots; covered with spines.

**Adult:** 2- to 2.5-inch wingspan. Outer third of wings orange with black border. Tip of front wings squared off. Resemble dead leaves. Favors northern latitudes and higher elevations.

**Habitat:** Marshes, streams, wet meadows.

**Range:** Northern two-thirds of U.S.; southern half of Canada.

**Comments:** One (north) to two (south) broods per year. Males perch.

**Winter strategy:** Adults hibernate, sometimes in groups of two or three.

**Caterpillar host plants:** Nettle.

**Adult food sources:** Various wildflowers, sap.

## Mourning Cloak (Nymphalis antiopa)

**Eggs:** White; laid in clusters of up to 250 around host plant twigs.

**Caterpillar:** Black with many white and orange spots; many black branching spines; red prolegs.

**Adult:** 3- to 3.5-inch wingspan. Dark, cream-edged wings marked with bright blue dots.

**Habitat:** Woodlands, forest openings and edges, wooded streams.

**Range:** U.S. and all but extreme northern Canada.

**Comments:** Usually single brooded. Males perch. Unusually long-lived, adults living ten to eleven months. One of earliest butterflies to appear in the spring. May estivate during summer hot spells.

**Winter strategy:** Hibernates as adult under loose slabs of bark or in hollow trees; often emerges on warm winter days.

**Caterpillar host plants:** Elm, poplar, willow.
**Adult food sources:** Meadow flowers, animal dung, rotting fruit.

## Baltimore (*Euphydryas phaeton*)

**Eggs:** Yellow; laid in clusters of one hundred to seven hundred.
**Caterpillar:** Black with orange stripes on sides and black branching spines. Young larvae move from lower leaves, where eggs were laid, to upper leaves, where they build a covered silk nest.
**Adult:** 1.5- to 2.5-inch wingspan. A singularly handsome butterfly, its dark wings bordered with red-orange, with rows of cream-colored dots inside this border.
**Habitat:** Wetlands, bogs, marshes, wet meadows.
**Range:** Eastern U.S. north of southern coastal states.
**Comments:** One brood per year. Males perch. Like the Baltimore Oriole, named for Lord Baltimore because its orange and black colors matched the colors of this seventeenth-century colonist's coat of arms.
**Winter strategy:** Larva hibernates in silk nest near ground.
**Caterpillar host plants:** Turtlehead, plantain, white ash, false foxglove.
**Adult food sources:** Milkweed, daisy, clover, viburnum, black-eyed susan, mud, dung.

## Pearl Crescent (*Phyciodes tharos*)

**Eggs:** Pale green, clusters of twenty to one hundred laid on underside of aster leaves. Females lay as many as seven hundred eggs.
**Caterpillar:** Chocolate brown with small, white spots; many brown, branching spines.
**Adult:** 1- to 1.5-inch wingspan. Orange with dark markings; suggests a small fritillary.
**Habitat:** Meadows, old fields, pastures, roadsides.
**Range:** East of Rockies, southwest to Southern California, and northwest to southern Alberta.
**Comments:** Two (north) to six (south) broods per year. Males patrol. One of the most common temperate butterflies.
**Winter strategy:** Hibernates as caterpillar.
**Caterpillar host plants:** Aster.

**Adult food sources:** Daisy, zinnia, clover, goldenrod, dandelion, yarrow, mint, oregano, milkweed.

## Great Spangled Fritillary (*Speyeria cybele*)

**Eggs:** Pale yellow; laid singly and randomly near violets, but not on them. Most eggs laid in late summer.
**Caterpillar:** Black, fuzzy, and covered with orange-based spines.
**Adult:** 2.5- to 3.5-inch wingspan. Large, orange butterfly with black dots, dashes, and crescents; shiny silver spots on underside of wings.
**Habitat:** Roadsides, fields, wet meadows, forest edges.
**Range:** Central North America, from East to West Coast.
**Comments:** One brood per year. Males patrol.
**Winter strategy:** First instar larva hibernates.
**Caterpillar host plants:** Violet.
**Adult food sources:** Milkweed, thistle, joe-pye weed, ironweed, and many other plants; dung.

## SNOUTS (Family Libytheidae)

## American Snout (*Libytheana carinenta*)

**Eggs:** Pale green; laid singly on young host plant leaves.
**Caterpillar:** Dark green with many small, yellow spots.
**Adult:** 1.5- to 2-inch wingspan. Mouthparts extended into snoutlike projection. Dark wings with orange splotches; white markings on front wings, which have squared-off tips.
**Habitat:** Woodlands and brushy areas, especially near water.
**Range:** Carolinas west to Southern California; sometimes occurs farther north.
**Comments:** One or two broods per year. Males perch. Only snout species in North America.
**Winter strategy:** Migratory; southern populations overwinter as adults.
**Caterpillar host plants:** Hackberry.
**Adult food sources:** Dogwood, peach, rabbitbrush, goldenrod, milkweed, mesquite.

# HARVESTERS, BLUES, COPPERS, AND HAIRSTREAKS (Family Lycaenidae)

## Harvester (Feniseca tarquinius)

**Eggs:** Pale green; laid singly among aphids.

**Caterpillar:** Gray with many hairs, but usually covered with aphid skins and silk.

**Adult:** 1- to 1.25-inch wingspan. Black wings with large orange patches.

**Habitat:** Woodlands, swamps.

**Range:** Eastern half of U.S.

**Comments:** Only North American butterfly with carnivorous caterpillars. Two broods per year. Males perch. Fast fliers.

**Winter strategy:** Probably overwinters as larva.

**Caterpillar host plants:** Insectivorous! Eats woolly aphids, which feed on alders, ash, beech, hawthorn, currant, and witch hazel.

**Adult food sources:** Adults do not drink nectar; they eat "honeydew" produced by aphids.

## Gray Hairstreak (Strymon melinus)

**Eggs:** Pale green; laid singly on host flowers.

**Caterpillar:** Small (.5 inch). Color variable, from tan to pink to reddish brown or green. Segments armored from above by platelike shell.

**Adult:** 1- to 1.25-inch wingspan. Gray with bright orange spot on outer corner of each hind wing.

**Habitat:** Open woods, roadsides, old fields, parks.

**Range:** U.S. and southern Canada.

**Comments:** Many broods each year. Males perch on hilltops. One of the most widely distributed butterflies.

**Winter strategy:** Pupa hibernates.

**Caterpillar host plants:** Legumes, corn, oak, mint, strawberry, mallow, cotton, pine, milkweed, to name just a few. This species is no doubt so successful because it uses such a variety of host species.

**Adult food sources:** Various wildflowers.

## American Copper (*Lycaena phlaeas*)

**Eggs:** Pale green; laid singly.

**Caterpillar:** Small (.5 inch). Variable color: red to yellow-green to green.

**Adult:** .75- to 1.25-inch wingspan. Bright orange front wings with black spots; bright red-orange band on end of each hind wing.

**Habitat:** Old fields, rights-of-way, vacant lots.

**Range:** Eastern U.S. and Canada north of Gulf states; north to Alaska.

**Comments:** Two broods per year. Males perch and patrol. Because larvae of this common species eat sheep sorrel, an introduced species from Europe, as its primary food, this is likely an introduced Old World species; consequently, some sources call it the Little Copper instead of American Copper.

**Winter strategy:** Larva hibernates.

**Caterpillar host plants:** Sheep sorrel.

**Adult food sources:** Coltsfoot, daisy, milkweed, cinquefoil.


## Spring Azure (*Celastrina argiolus*)

**Eggs:** Pale green with white ridges; laid singly on host plant flowers and buds.

**Caterpillar:** Green, yellow, or reddish brown with dark stripes on top.

**Adult:** Beautiful, small, dainty blue butterfly. Bluish lavender wings; front wings bordered with narrow black band.

**Habitat:** Woodlands, forest openings and edges, swamps.

**Range:** Most of U.S. and Canada north to Alaska; absent from most of Texas.

**Comments:** One or two broods per year. Among the first to fly in spring. Males perch. Larvae eat flowers and fruits; different broods eat different foods. Related Pygmy Blue (*Brephidium exilis*) of southwestern U.S., with a wingspan of less than .5 inch, is the smallest butterfly in the world.

**Winter strategy:** Overwinters as pupa.

**Caterpillar host plants:** Dogwood, cherry, sumac, meadowsweet, apple, oak, legumes.

**Adult food sources:** Redbud, serviceberry, spicebush, blackberry, milkweed, clover, dung, mud.

## SKIPPERS (Family Hesperiidae)

### Silver-Spotted Skipper (Epargyreus clarus)

**Eggs:** Green with red cap; laid singly on top of host plant leaves.

**Caterpillar:** All skipper caterpillars have a distinctive shape: huge head, narrow first thoracic segment, which appears to be a neck, followed by a wide abdomen that tapers to the rear. Yellow-green body ringed by fine dark lines; large, dark head with orange spots at each antenna; very narrow "neck"; prolegs yellow, true legs red. Young caterpillars live inside a folded, silked-together host leaf; older caterpillars silk together several leaves.

**Adult:** 1.5- to 2.5-inch wingspan. Adults dull with drab orange spots on upper surface of front wings and large silver spots on undersurface of hind wings.

**Habitat:** Open fields, yards, rights-of-way, second-growth woodlands.

**Range:** Most of U.S.

**Comments:** Two to three broods per year. Males perch. Named for rapid, "skipping" flight. Mimic leaves by hanging upside down from vegetation in afternoon.

**Winter strategy:** Overwinters as pupa.

**Caterpillar host plants:** Black locust, wisteria, kudzu, and other legumes.

**Adult food sources:** Ironweed, clovers, dogbane, joe-pye weed.

## SPHINX OR HAWK MOTHS (Family Sphingidae)

### Hummingbird Clearwing Moth (Hemaris thysbe)

**Eggs:** Green, spherical; laid singly on leaves of host plant.

**Caterpillar:** Bright green and fleshy, with a yellow stripe along both sides of the center dorsal line. Like most members of the family, has a harmless but harsh-looking "horn" extending from the last abdominal segment, hence the general name hornworm for caterpillars in this family, which includes the Tomato Hornworm, the large, fleshy, green caterpillar common in vegetable gardens.

**Adult:** 1.75- to 2.25-inch wingspan. Scaleless, transparent patch on each front wing, hence the name. Many other members of this family also confused with hummingbirds; some have brightly colored hind wings and/or colorful bands on abdomen.

**Habitat:** Fields, forest edges.

**Range:** Eastern U.S. and Canada.

**Comments:** One (north) or two (south) broods per year. Diurnal. Hover at flowers, where they sip nectar through uncurled proboscis. Often mistaken for a "baby" hummingbird.

**Winter strategy:** Overwinters as cocoon in leaf litter.

**Caterpillar host plants:** Viburnum, buck brush, hawthorn, honeysuckle, apple, cherry.

**Adult food sources:** Milkweed, bee balm, lilac, and many other flowers.

---

## GIANT SILKWORM MOTHS (Family Saturniidae)

### Luna Moth *(Actias luna)*

**Eggs:** White; laid singly or in small groups on both surfaces of host plant leaves.

**Caterpillar:** Large (3 inches), fleshy lime green with pale stripes on side; turns reddish brown just before pupating.

**Adult:** 4-inch wingspan. Pale green with eyespots and long, sweeping tails. Spring broods marked with pink or purple wing margins; summer broods have yellow wing margins.

**Habitat:** Woodlands and forest edges.

**Range:** Eastern half of U.S. and Canada.

**Comments:** One (north) to three (south) broods. Calling time around midnight. Attracted to lights.

**Winter strategy:** Overwinters as cocoon on ground in leaf litter, often at base of host plant.

**Caterpillar host plants:** Hickory, cherry, beech, pecan, alder, willow, sweet gum, persimmon, sumac, white birch (in north).

**Adult food sources:** Short-lived adult form has reduced mouthparts and does not eat.

## Cecropia Moth (Hyalophora cecropia)

**Eggs:** Rows of two to six laid on both sides of host plant leaves.

**Caterpillar:** Large, green, and fleshy with small, colorful appendages (scoli) along body; dorsal scoli yellow, lateral scoli blue, those near head orange. Young larvae gregarious; older larvae solitary.

**Adult:** 4- to 6-inch wingspan. Female Cecropia is largest moth in North America. Reddish body with white collar and bands on abdomen. Large antennae. Reddish marginal bands and crescent-shaped eyespots on each wing.

**Habitat:** Woodlands and forest edges.

**Range:** East of Rockies in U.S. and Canada; three closely related and similar species inhabit the continent west of the Rockies.

**Comments:** One brood per year. Calling time 3 A.M. to sunrise. Attracted to lights.

**Winter strategy:** Overwinters as cocoon attached lengthwise to twigs.

**Caterpillar host plants:** Apple, ash, beech, birch, elm, maple, poplar, white oak, willow.

**Adult food sources:** Short-lived adult form has reduced mouthparts and does not eat.

## Polyphemus Moth (Antheraea polyphemus)

**Eggs:** Off-white with dark band around the middle; laid singly or in rows of two or three on host plant leaves.

**Caterpillar:** Large (3 inches), bright green, fleshy; pale yellow vertical bands between segments. Similar to Luna caterpillar but lacks lateral stripe.

**Adult:** 3.5- to 5.5-inch wingspan. Brown wings with large eyespots on hind wings.

**Habitat:** Woodlands.

**Range:** U.S. and southern Canada; not known from Nevada or Arizona.

**Comments:** One (north) to two (south) broods per year. Calling times 11 P.M. to 1 A.M. and 3:30 A.M. to dawn.

**Winter strategy:** Overwinters as cocoon attached to food plants.

**Caterpillar host plants:** Ash, birch, grape, hickory, maple, oak, pine, apple.

**Adult food sources:** Short-lived adult form has reduced mouthparts and does not eat.

# Royal Walnut Moth (Citheronia regalis)

**Eggs:** Laid singly or in groups of two or three on both sides of host plant leaves. Larvae visible through eggshell just before hatching.

**Caterpillar:** Spectacularly huge, up to 6 inches. Ferocious looking but harmless; called Hickory Horned Devil. Large thoracic horns are not stingers, though tips of abdominal spines might pierce skin; horns and spines may discourage avian predators from trying to swallow these caterpillars. Green with pale yellow bars on each segment. Horns disproportionately large on all instars. Shakes head violently when disturbed.

**Adult:** 4- to 6-inch wingspan; large handsome orange moth with many yellow spots.

**Habitat:** Woodlands and forest edges.

**Range:** Eastern U.S. from east Texas through central Missouri, north to southern Michigan and Massachusetts.

**Comments:** One brood per year. Calling time 9:30 P.M. to midnight. Caterpillar was known nearly seventy years before adult moth was described in 1793.

**Winter strategy:** Cocoon, which may last two winters.

**Caterpillar host plants:** Walnut, sumac, persimmon, lilac, ash, cotton, gum, hickory, sycamore.

**Adult food sources:** Short-lived adult form has reduced mouthparts and does not eat.


# Io Moth (Automeris io)

**Eggs:** Oblong with flat top; suggest small, yellow corn kernels; laid in clusters on host plant leaves.

**Caterpillar:** Green and fleshy with brown-bordered white lateral stripe; many branched green appendages (scoli) with many stinging spines. *Do not handle this caterpillar!*

**Adult:** 2- to 3-inch wingspan. Males golden, females browner. Both sexes have huge eyespots on hind wings.

**Habitat:** Woodlands and forest edges.

**Range:** Eastward from the Great Plains and southern Canada.

**Comments:** One (north) to three (south) broods per year. Calling time dusk to midnight.

**Winter strategy:** Overwinters as cocoon.

**Caterpillar host plants:** Redbud, hackberry, cherry, sassafras, birch, clover, corn, elm, maple, oak, willow; preferred foods vary geographically.

**Adult food sources:** Short-lived adult form has reduced mouthparts and does not eat.

---

## TIGER MOTHS (Family Arctiidae)

### Isabella Tiger Moth *(Pyrrharctia isabella)*

**Eggs:** Cream to pale yellow; pinpoint size; laid in clusters of thirty to two hundred, often multilayered, on underside of host leaves.

**Caterpillar:** Fuzzy with wide rusty and black bands, known as Woolly Bear. Similar black, hairy caterpillar with red rings between segments is larva of Great Leopard Moth.

**Adult:** 2- to 2.25-inch wingspan. Dull yellow-orange wings. Nondescript; seldom noticed.

**Habitat:** Forest edges, roadsides.

**Range:** U.S. and southern Canada.

**Comments:** Two broods per year.

**Winter strategy:** Overwinters as Woolly Bear caterpillar, which rolls into ball in leaf litter, brush pile, or woodpile. Pupates in spring.

**Caterpillar host plants:** Aster, birch, clover, corn, elm, maple, sunflower, and many others.

**Adult food sources:** Does not feed, but does drink water condensed on leaves.

### Fall Webworm Moth *(Hyphantria cunea)*

**Eggs:** Laid en masse on undersides of host plant leaves.

**Caterpillar:** Variable: green to black with yellow or orange markings on sides; clusters of very long, fine, silky hairs radiate from each segment.

**Adult:** 1- to 1.5-inch wingspan. White wings; front wings marked with dark spots.

**Habitat:** Forest edges, roadsides, backyards.

**Range:** Eastern two-thirds of U.S. and Canada.

**Comments:** One (north) or two (south) broods per year. Larvae build webs in outer branches of trees in late summer and fall; because most plant growth is finished by this time, webworms are more unsightly than harmful.

**Winter strategy:** Overwinters as pupa.

**Caterpillar host plants:** Many trees and shrubs, including ash, hickory, maple, oak, walnut, apple.

**Adult food sources:** Mouthparts poorly developed; do not feed, but can sip free water.

## TENT CATERPILLAR MOTHS
## (Family Lasiocampidae)

### Eastern Tent Caterpillar Moth *(Malacosma americanum)*

**Eggs:** Hardened masses laid on host plant twigs.

**Caterpillar:** Hairy, bluish larvae eaten by cuckoos, tanagers, and orioles.

**Adult:** 1- to 1.75-inch wingspan. Drab, nondescript light brown moth. Upon emerging, females releases a sex pheromone that attracts males; mating and egg-laying follow quickly; adult moths die after eggs are laid, often with twenty-four hours of emerging.

**Habitat:** Forest edges, roadsides.

**Range:** Eastern three-quarters of U.S. and Canada; a western species occurs in California.

**Comments:** One brood per year. Population cyclic—builds for several years, then crashes. Larvae create unsightly web tents in forks of trees and shrubs in spring. Not to be confused with Fall Webworms, which build webs in outer branches of trees in late summer and fall.

**Winter strategy:** Overwinters as egg stage.

**Caterpillar host plants:** Many trees and shrubs, especially cherry, apple, and crab apple.

**Adult food sources:** Short-lived adult form has reduced mouthparts and does not eat.

## TUSSOCK MOTHS (Family Lymantriidae)

### Gypsy Moth (*Lymantria dispar*)

**Eggs:** Conspicuous tan-colored egg cases cemented to tree trunks, where they spend the winter.

**Caterpillar:** Hairy body marked with red and blue spots. Eaten by cuckoos, tanagers, and orioles.

**Adult:** 1.25- to 2.5-inch wingspan. Sexually dimorphic; females much bigger and lighter than males. Light to white in color, with small black spots on wings. Adults seldom seen.

**Habitat:** Deciduous woodlands.

**Range:** Spreading inexorably westward from East Coast.

**Comments:** Intentionally released in 1868 in Massachusetts for silk production; great example of danger of releasing exotic species. During population explosions, caterpillars rain frass (droppings) from treetops onto forest floor.

**Winter strategy:** Overwinters as egg case on tree trunk.

**Caterpillar host plants:** Oak favored (hence their destruction of eastern deciduous forests), but also apple, birch, box elder, willow.

**Adult food sources:** Short-lived adult form has reduced mouthparts and does not eat.

# CHAPTER 4

# Gardening for Butterflies

Combining a love of butterflies with a love of gardening seems like a natural marriage. Butterflies and wildflowers complement each other. Wildflowers provide the energy-rich nectar butterflies require; in return, butterflies help pollinate the flowers they visit. It's part of nature's balance.

The butterfly-wildflower symbiosis is one most people welcome in their backyards, and many folks plant wildflower gardens to attract butterflies. Often, however, their success is limited. People plant extensive gardens of nectar-producing wildflowers but attract few butterflies. A few adults may flutter by, but that hardly seems a just reward for all the time, effort, and expense that went into the garden.

The reason there are few butterflies, in spite of lavish butterfly gardens, is that gardeners tend to focus solely on the beautiful, showy adults—the typically short-lived adult butterflies. But in order to have butterflies, you must first have caterpillars. Thus managing habitat for butterflies requires that you manage it for caterpillars. And often the plants caterpillars eat are not the same ones that produce the adults' favorite nectars. Even though butterflies may sip nectar from a variety of sources, many species have specific requirements for the caterpillars' host plants. Females lay their eggs, or oviposit, only on the appropriate host plants, which often are limited to just a handful of related species. Monarchs, for example, oviposit only on members of the milkweed family, Red Admirals choose nettles, and Painted Ladies lay their eggs on thistles. Without these "weeds," these butterflies cannot and will not reproduce. To attract residential populations of breeding butterflies to your backyard, you must provide caterpillar food as well as nectar.

The rub is that caterpillar food plants are often weedy and less spectacular than the nectar producers that make showy garden plants. Nettles, thistles, plantains, grasses, and a variety of trees and shrubs are among the most important caterpillar foods, and anyone who wants to attract butter-flies should plant at least some of these in the backyard.

## PLANT VARIETIES

It's important to maintain a balance between nectar plants and caterpillar food plants. If you feed the caterpillars but don't provide nectar, the adult butterflies will leave. Conversely, if you ignore the caterpillars but plant lots of nectar producers, you'll see only an occasional butterfly flutter by.

Select caterpillar host plants based on the species of butterflies you hope to attract. To give you a feel for who eats what, here are some common butterflies and the plants their caterpillars eat: Tiger Swallowtail (tulip poplar, black cherry), Spicebush Swallowtail (sassafras, spicebush), fritil-laries (violets), Question Marks (nettles), Mourning Cloaks (willow, birch, elm), Red Admiral (nettles), Painted Lady (thistle), Buckeye (snapdragons, plantains), Monarch (milkweed). See Appendix B for a more complete list of caterpillar host plants.

Adult butterflies are less selective about which plants provide their nectar. Many butterfly books include lists of dozens of nectar-bearing species, and I've included a more complete list in Appendix A, but here are a handful of plants that are butterfly magnets and are native to North America. Conspicuously absent are non-native species such as butterfly bush (*Buddleia davidii*) and purple loosestrife (*Lythrum salicaria*), even though butterfly bush is universally touted as the ultimate nectar source for butterflies. Why I don't recommend these species is explained in the chapter on conservation.

Plant just a few of these wildflowers to turn your backyard into a nec-tar bar: common milkweed (*Asclepias syriaca*), butterfly weed (*A. tuberosa*), swamp milkweed (*A. incarnata*), joe-pye weed (*Eupatorium* spp.), ironweed (*Vernonia* spp.), lantana (*Lantana* spp.), purple coneflower (*Echinacea pur-purea*), asters (*Aster* spp.), black-eyed susans (*Rudbeckia hirta*), sunflowers (*Helianthus* spp.), blazing star (*Liatris* spp.), trumpet honeysuckle (*Lonicera sempervirens*), and Dutchman's pipe (*Aristolochia macrophylla*). As a bonus, you'll also be delighted when you discover that hummingbirds use the nec-tar garden as much as the butterflies.

It's best to plant your garden in the fall. Transplants acclimate to the soil and local conditions over the winter, and growth is rapid and vigorous the following spring. Spring plantings often get off to a slow start and don't prosper until the following year.

## PLANNING THE GARDEN

Plan your garden for an open, sunny location, which most butterflies prefer. Select a variety of species, types, and sizes of plants. A mix of herbaceous flowers, vines, shrubs, and trees will attract the greatest variety of species. Plant flowers in bunches rather than singly. A large patch of color attracts even butterflies passing by at considerable height. And plan your garden so that the taller plants are toward the back and the smaller plants are in front. This will allow you the best chance to see all the butterflies that enter the garden.

I prefer buying mature, native perennials that will flower the same year I plant them. That way the caterpillars and butterflies can use the leaves and nectar, and I get to enjoy the flowers. A perennial garden almost maintains itself. The trick is getting started.

If you've got more money than time, you might want to have a butterfly garden planned for you. Sketch a map of your backyard, and take it to a local garden center. Find an employee who enjoys butterflies as much as you do and explain your goals. Be prepared to spend several hundred dollars for the plants you'll need. Budget a lot more if you plan to have the garden center do the landscaping.

Whatever your budget, butterfly gardening is doable. You can start small with just a few plants and add a few more each year. If you're on a limited budget, start with butterfly weed, joe-pye weed, ironweed, and blazing star. I promise your summers will never be the same.

A lazy and inexpensive way to cultivate a butterfly garden is to mow less often, and mow a smaller portion of the yard. Let nature take its course. Birds and mice will plant the seeds, and natural plant succession will dictate the species composition of the garden. But this takes time; a natural garden may take years to be productive. Many of the grasses and weeds that mature in these unmown areas will provide caterpillar food. If you live in an ecologically backward community that enforces antiweed ordinances, make sure your natural garden cannot be seen from the street.

Keep the use of herbicides and pesticides to a minimum. This is essential. People who routinely treat their yards with chemicals won't see butterflies. Insecticides kill insects, and that includes butterflies. This is also true of organic pesticides. BT (*Bacillus thuringensis*) is a favorite "natural" pesticide often used for gypsy moth control, but it kills virtually any caterpillar that ingests it. BT doesn't discriminate between the good and bad species. Herbicides kill caterpillar food plants, and that's just as bad as not planting them in the first place.

If you have weed or insect problems, treat the plants individually. Clip or dig up any plants you want eliminated. If you do use herbicides, spray them only on the offending plants rather than treat the entire backyard. Better yet, use natural insecticides such as liquid detergents. You don't want to spend a lot of time and money cultivating a beautiful flower garden only to drive off or poison the butterflies with chemicals. A backyard shouldn't look like a golf course. If it does, you won't see many butterflies.

## SOURCES OF WILDFLOWERS

Planting a garden of native plants requires a source of wildflowers. Private landowners frown on trespassers stealing their plants, and it's illegal to uproot plants in parks and other public places. If you're the patient sort, you can collect seeds of desirable species along roadsides and even in public parks. If you have friends with enviable butterfly gardens, ask for sprigs or small plants. Most gardeners are wonderfully generous.

If you want to buy plants for your garden, be careful where you shop. Look for wild stock. Many garden centers and even some nurseries have responded to the demand for native plants, but they often sell propagated varieties that may yield little nectar. They've been bred for their appearance rather than their ecological value. I prefer to buy plants at nature centers such as Beechwood Farms in Pittsburgh and Bowman's Hill Wildflower Preserve in New Hope, Pennsylvania. At these and many other nature centers around the country, staff and volunteer naturalists propagate wild native plants and sell them each year as a fund-raiser. Interest in native plants is growing, and many sell their entire stock on the first day of the sale.

Another source for native species is a growing number of nurseries that specialize in promoting natural landscapes. Most are small and locally oriented, so ask around at nature centers, state parks, and progressive garden centers. If your favorite garden center doesn't have what you're looking for, ask the store manager to recommend a nearby native nursery. Or do an Internet search for "butterfly gardens," "butterfly conservation," "native plants," "native vegetation," "native nectar-bearing plants," or "native plants for butterflies." This will yield volumes of information, mail-order sources, and places you might actually be able to visit.

I strongly recommend the use of native plants. In the long run, natural gardens not only will be more ecologically responsible, but also will be easier to maintain and cheaper to create. Because natives are adapted to local conditions, they grow and prosper vigorously. Once established, they can easily be separated and transplanted at minimal cost. For more information on natives, see page 63.

## BASKING PERCHES

Like all insects, butterflies are ectothermic; that is, their body temperatures vary with that of the surrounding environment. That's why you often see butterflies basking in the sun early in the morning. They are warming their bodies by absorbing heat from warm areas such as concrete and gravel driveways and walkways, wooden decks, and retaining walls.

You can use this behavior to add another element to your butterfly garden. Large rocks make excellent basking perches. Place them in south-facing open areas to maximize their heat-gathering ability. Plant caterpillar host species and nectar-bearing flowers among a patch of scattered rocks to create a colorful rock garden. Use low-growing species so they won't cast cooling shadows on the rocks.

## WATER AND MUD SOURCES

Your butterfly garden should also have a source of water. Though butterflies sometimes stop to drink at birdbaths and other water features, a subtle approach to water can be more effective. A large rock with a shallow depression can collect morning dew and the spray from a mister set up near a birdbath. Another option is to fill a birdbath or large flowerpot saucer with stones and water. Butterflies will tiptoe on the stones while sipping the water that lies beneath. Even a saucer filled with a muddy mixture of soil and water appeals to some butterflies. Use whatever materials are readily available. You'll discover that butterflies enjoy water sources as much as birds do.

Another reason to try the mud puddle technique is that many butterflies obtain nutrients and minerals from muddy areas. Tiger Swallowtails commonly "puddle" by the dozens, gathering along streamside puddles in the spring and summer to sip moisture. Sometimes they even extract nutrients by puddling on cow manure and other deposits of animal waste.

Sulphurs, whites, blues, and skippers are also common puddlers. Young males that haven't yet found mates often puddle in large groups to obtain the nutrients and minerals required for reproduction.

## BUTTERFLY FEEDERS

Butterflies can also be attracted to nectar feeders. Make a butterfly feeder by filling a shallow container, such as a plastic flowerpot saucer, with hummingbird nectar (one part table sugar, fours parts water). Add a handful of multicolored plastic kitchen scouring pads. Butterflies don't like to get their feet wet, so they will perch on the scouring pads, extend their proboscises through the mesh, and sip the nectar. Place this feeder in a shaded spot so the nectar doesn't ferment too quickly. And be advised that this will also attract ants, bees, and wasps.

There are also commercially available butterfly feeders, which are similar to hummingbird feeders. Look for them at nature centers, wild bird stores, and garden centers. Though there's no reason they shouldn't attract butterflies, I've had no luck with these feeders.

Butterflies also like rotting fruit. A saucer with a few pieces of overripe banana works well. As the fruit softens with decay, a variety of butterflies will visit to sip the juices. Again, expect other insects to show up for the handout, so keep these feeders away from areas where you spend a lot of time.

If you're really ambitious, whip up a batch of mung for your butterflies. In *Enjoying Butterflies More,* author Jeffrey Glassberg recommends a recipe he credits to Don Riepe. To a base of molasses, add overripe bananas and other rotting fruit if it's available. Then add enough beer to make the concoction spreadable. Let it sit for a few days in a covered container, then smear it on deeply furrowed tree bark or place a few tablespoons in a shallow dish. Anglewings, tortoiseshells, satyrs, and other butterflies that favor sap and rotting fruit may visit a mung feeder.

## BUTTERFLY SHELTERS

Butterfly boxes have become popular items at garden centers in recent years. The idea is that the butterflies that overwinter as adults can sometimes be coaxed into butterfly boxes as an artificial hibernaculum. Some butterflies hibernate in hollow logs and tree cavities and behind loose slabs of bark on dead trees. Here their delicate wings are protected from wind, rain, and snow. A few species *might* possibly use a butterfly box as a winter refuge. But don't count on it. I've never found a butterfly in a butterfly box, and I've had two up for more than ten years. But wasps love them. Each year mine are filled with nests of paper wasps. And I wouldn't be surprised to find a beehive in there someday.

Most butterfly boxes are roughly 8-by-8-by-18-inch artificial cavities that can be mounted on a post or attached to a tree. A series of $1/2$-by-3-inch vertical slots on the front of the box provide access. It is recommended that a long piece of tree bark be placed inside the box to give the butterflies a perch. But have realistic expectations: Showy, colorful species such as Monarchs and swallowtails do not use butterfly boxes. Anglewings, Mourning Cloaks, Eastern Commas, or Question Marks might. Regard a butterfly house more as a garden ornament than a butterfly magnet.

A better, more natural butterfly shelter is a woodpile. You'll need a supply of logs 3 to 5 feet long. Begin with a foundation of logs 6 to 12 inches apart, about as long as the logs are, to form a square pile. Place each succeeding layer of logs perpendicular to the previous one to build a crisscross stack of logs 3 to 5 feet high. Stacking the logs loosely will provide plenty of roosting space. Cover the top with a piece of plywood or a tarp, and anchor this roof with a final layer of logs. Build the shelter in a spot shaded by deciduous trees so that resting butterflies will not bake under the summer sun. In the winter, when trees are bare, the sun warms the shelter.

# CHAPTER 5

# Conservation

Butterflies and moths are indicators of environmental health, reminiscent of the proverbial canary in the coal mine. If Monarchs, Luna Moths, or even Cabbage Whites disappear, conservation-minded citizens wonder why. Is habitat being destroyed by a new housing development? Has the power company or highway department recently sprayed a nearby right-of-way?

For every environmental impact, there is an equal environmental reaction. Negative impacts have negative consequences. Monitoring butterfly and moth populations is just one way backyard naturalists can keep their fingers on the environment's pulse.

Conservation is often perceived to be organized by governmental agencies or private environmental groups, but effective butterfly conservation can also be practiced in backyards all across the continent. Though postage-stamp-size suburban backyards may seem too small to make a difference, millions of small backyards add up to a major conservation effort. Throw in larger backyards and rural properties, and homeowners can set aside millions of acres for butterfly conservation. You can help butterflies not only by joining conservation organizations throughout North America and the world (see Appendix E), but also by employing conservation practices at home.

## AVOID CHEMICALS

The most important and easiest step we can take to help butterflies is to stop using herbicides and pesticides in the backyard. According to the National Audubon Society, Americans apply 67 million pounds of pesticides to backyards every year. If we add school yards and golf courses into the mix, the total increases to 73 million pounds. On a global scale, the annual amount of pesticides applied is about 5 billion pounds.

Though it is arguably necessary to use chemicals to feed the world (though I'm sure organic farmers would beg to differ), there is simply no reason to contaminate our backyards with toxic chemicals. But we've bought into the notion that the only acceptable backyard is one where every leaf, twig, and blade of grass is perfect. So we strive for perfection by applying fertilizers, herbicides, fungicides, and insecticides from the beginning of the growing season until the first frost.

But in the process, we kill much more than the pests. We destroy the beneficial soil microbes, insects, and birds. We sicken our pets and even our children. And yes, we kill the caterpillars and then complain because we see no butterflies.

The pathway to safer, healthier backyards and more butterflies is to lower our standards a bit. Tolerate and even embrace an imperfect lawn, and welcome a few more weeds and insects. Contrary to popular opinion, most insects are benign or beneficial. Only a few are truly pests. And those you can control by hand or with environmentally safer insecticidal soaps. And think of all the money you'll save. Herbicides and insecticides are very expensive. Take the savings and buy native plants for caterpillars and butterflies.

If you live in a rural area, your property may be sprayed without your knowledge or permission. Here in West Virginia, the Department of Highways routinely sprays roadsides to control weeds. One year I watched the late-summer crop of Monarch caterpillars die as the offending vegetation wilted.

Don't tolerate this unhealthy intrusion on your private property. Contact your local highway office, ask if roadside vegetation is controlled with chemicals, then ask how to go about sparing your road frontage the insult. In the county where I live, I've completed a form denoting my road frontage as a "no-spray" zone. It seems the state should be required to notify property owners and ask permission to spray toxic chemicals on private land. But at least in West Virginia, there's a mechanism in place for landowners to limit the state's penchant for spraying. If your state lacks a similar procedure, contact your state legislators and demand protection. This can be an uphill struggle, because the bureaucrats who administer these roadside maintenance programs have been taught to use chemicals to solve plant problems.

## USE NATIVE SPECIES

Gardening is the number one leisure activity in America, and we have been convinced by the gardening industry that exotic plants and specially bred horticultural varieties are best for designing landscapes and backyards. We want plants that are free from insect pests, plants that are hardy and fast-growing, plants that outcompete native "weeds" that might otherwise take over our yards. This rationale seems to make perfect sense, but only because we've failed to consider the ecological implications of managing millions of small backyards.

The total amount of backyard habitat in this country is staggering. Though apartment dwellers may only maintain a window box or two, quarter-acre lots are common, and in an affluent society such as ours, many people maintain backyards that encompass several acres. According to the *1998 Statistical Abstract of the United States,* American backyards total at least 35 million acres. That's more than 50,000 square miles of backyard habitat. Unfortunately, the typical American homeowner has been brainwashed to believe that backyards, regardless of size, must be sprayed, mowed, and manicured into submission.

Wake up, America! Weedy, overgrown backyards dominated by native plant species are great for butterflies, birds, bats, and other backyard beasts, and they require less attention and expense. Just maintain minimal open space for a vegetable garden, picnicking, a play area for the kids, and some room to walk around. In larger yards, connect these areas with a system of mowed trails.

Ecologists estimate conservatively that fifty thousand non-native plant species have been intentionally or accidentally introduced into the United States. Of those, about five thousand have established themselves as part of the wild plant communities, and many have become invasive. Multiflora rose, kudzu, autumn olive, purple loosestrife, and Asian bittersweet come immediately to mind. Invasive species spread rapidly and dominate the landscape because they outcompete natives for sunlight and nutrients. Some degrade aquatic habitats by promoting soil erosion. Some decrease the diversity of microorganisms in the soil. Some compete so aggressively and successfully that they harm endangered native species. In other words, invasive exotic plants wreak havoc on native plant communities. And we are responsible for this ecological disruption because we fail to discourage exotics.

One facet of invasions by exotic plant species that has received little attention from ecologists is the ecological impact of exotics replacing natives. Specifically, we know little about the effects of this transition on the food habits of plant-eating insects and higher predators such as birds that eat those insects. In the summer of 2001, Doug Tallamy, an entomologist at the University of Delaware who is concerned about the impact of exotic plants on native insects, did some preliminary fieldwork to investigate these effects.

The vast majority of plant-eating insects are specialists and eat only a few closely related groups of plants (for example, Monarch caterpillars eat only milkweeds, and fritillaries require violets). These relationships have evolved over long periods of time, which has allowed the insects to adapt to various physical and physiological defenses, such as thorns or toxins. Consequently, native plant-eating insects can efficiently use their preferred host plant's tissues as an energy source.

Insects that are specialized to eat one related group of plants do not have the ability to efficiently and effectively consume unrelated plant species. Exotic species are unknown to our native plant-eating insects, so most insects are not able to consume their tissues. Tallamy predicts that as invasive plant species come to dominate a landscape, native insects will be unable to use the solar energy stored by these exotic plants. Over time, that is devastating for native plant-eating insects, including lepidopteran caterpillars, and the predators that eat these insects, such as fish, frogs, toads, snakes, birds, bats, and many small mammals. Invasive plants such as multiflora rose, purple loosestrife, and kudzu have the potential to disrupt entire food chains and native ecosystems.

Tallamy formulated a field experiment to test the hypothesis that native herbivorous insects eat more native plant material than exotic plant material. He examined and quantified the amount of leaf area consumed by insects on both native and exotic plants. The results are striking and sure to stimulate more fieldwork on this fascinating ecological problem that has, until now, been ignored.

In every test, local plant-eating insects consumed significantly more plant tissue from native plant species than from exotics. This was true regardless of plant type—herbaceous, vine, or woody—and habitat. Among native plants, not all were equally palatable. This supports the notion that different groups of plant-eating insects prefer distinct types of plants.

The implications of this fieldwork on the management of backyard habitats and landscape design are enormous. Over time, invasive plants have the potential to alter not only the species composition and diversity of plant communities, but also an entire ecosystem's flow of energy by disrupting the interconnected food chains at every level. If plant-eating insects adapted to native species disappear as invasive plants take over a landscape, the frogs, toads, birds, and small mammals that eat those insects will be in jeopardy as well.

As a result of Tallamy's fieldwork, he has adopted a zero-tolerance approach to planting non-native species in backyard habitats. I've concluded that this is sound advice, and contrary to what you'll read in just about every other butterfly book, I encourage all butterfly gardeners to "go native."

## PARTICIPATE IN CITIZEN SCIENCE

There is little doubt that the star of the butterfly world is the Monarch. It's beautiful, it's commonly found across North America, and it's familiar to anyone who has ever even glanced at the butterflies that visit the backyard. But I suspect the Monarch's primary appeal is a trait it shares with the colorful Neotropical migrants of the bird world: Monarchs migrate.

In the years since the mystery of Monarch migration was unraveled back in 1975 by Dr. Fred Urquhart, the Monarch's migration and overwintering habits have captured the fancy of legions of lepidopterists, amateurs and professionals alike. A 1976 article in *National Geographic* by Dr. Urquhart entitled "Found at Last: The Monarch's Winter Home" ignited the public's interest, and many articles and books have followed in the intervening years.

Perhaps the most important result of the public's interest in Monarchs has been the founding of Monarch Watch by Dr. O. R. "Chip" Taylor, an insect ecologist at the University of Kansas. Monarch Watch is a citizen science project that allows anyone with an interest in Monarchs to participate in scientific research. For a small fee, participants get a supply of numbered, self-adhesive labels, which they apply to the wings of captured or homegrown late-summer Monarchs. In the wintering areas in Mexico, locals are paid a small bounty for tags they collect from dead butterflies. This serves as an incentive for the local people to protect the Monarch forest preserves rather than cut the trees for lumber or firewood.

Under normal circumstances, the return rate is low, because relatively few of the tens of millions of Monarchs that winter in Mexico die, and even fewer are tagged and found. For example, from 1996 through 1998, Pat Sutton, a naturalist at New Jersey's Cape May Bird Observatory, and a group of volunteers tagged nearly seventeen thousand monarchs. In the spring of 1999, they learned that six of their butterflies had been found and reported from a Mexican roost site. That's a return rate of just 0.035 percent

But when weather in the butterfly sanctuaries turns cold and wet, many Monarchs die, and more tags are recovered. Late in the winter of 2002, a freak combination of snow and cold rain hit the Monarch wintering grounds, and millions of Monarchs perished. The good news was that many tags were found among the dead.

Tom Pawlesh, a friend from Jefferson Hills, Pennsylvania, near Pittsburgh, received notice from Monarch Watch that four of the two hundred Monarchs he had tagged in September 2001 were found at the Monarch reserves in March 2002. That's a return rate of 2 percent. Each had traveled almost 1,900 miles from Tom's backyard. Other tagged Monarchs that year had traveled more than 2,300 miles to their Mexican wintering grounds.

Because of the efforts of Monarch Watch participants, entomologists have gained a better understanding of the Monarch's natural history. To learn more about Monarchs and become part of this fascinating citizen science program, contact Monarch Watch, Entomology Program, 1200 Sunnyside Avenue, University of Kansas, Lawrence, KS 66045, telephone 888-TAGGING, or visit its website at www.monarchwatch.org. For a modest annual membership fee, you get detailed information about Monarchs, a tagging kit, and complete instructions. It's a great way to introduce kids to science, insects, and natural history.

## PROTECT LEPIDOPTERAN HABITAT

Beyond our own backyards, the best conservation measure we can take for butterflies is to protect habitat for both caterpillars and adult lepidopterans. Any natural area set aside for any reason also serves as butterfly habitat. Parks, cemeteries, greenways, conservancy areas, state and national forests, state game lands, and wildlife management areas, though set aside for other purposes, such as recreation, open space, timber production, or the preservation of endangered species, also provide vast amounts of butterfly habitat, especially those with an abundance of native vegetation. Visit these places and enjoy their butterflies.

Effective conservation demands active participation. Lobby state agencies to include butterflies in their land management plans. Purchase a hunting or fishing license. Even if you never use it, it gives you the right to be heard by those who manage wildlife and seldom consider the effects of their decisions on butterflies. Membership in conservation organizations is certainly helpful, but it is those who attend public meetings, write letters, and call decision makers who make the greatest impact.

## BUTTERFLY FARMING

For centuries, butterflies have been collected for esthetic as well as scientific reasons. There has long been a flourishing trade in large, beautiful butterflies and moths. These colorful lepidopterans adorn the walls of homes and offices around the world. The species in greatest demand are the largest, showiest ones native to tropical rain forests and other endangered habitats. Larger species tend to reproduce at a slow rate, so over time, the butterfly trade has taken a serious toll on these most beautiful species. The rarer they have become, the greater their value to collectors.

Simply calling on common sense to protect something rarely seems to work. "If you collect all the butterflies in any given area," protectionists warned, "there will soon be no butterflies at all." But collectors and poachers tend to live for today and not think about tomorrow.

It's difficult to criticize native collectors and poachers. These are humans living at subsistence levels in some of the most undeveloped areas of the world. Collecting butterflies generates far more income than subsistence farming and hunting. Selling conservation to people struggling to feed their families from day to day is a difficult task.

A workable strategy for butterfly conservation in many parts of the world has been to treat butterflies as a renewable resource. Local people who traditionally practiced subsistence agriculture and cut tropical forests for fuel and lumber can now protect valuable habitats while raising butterflies to sell to collectors. Give people a practical reason to protect tropical forests and native wildlife, and they will. Raising a renewable crop such as butterflies provides a much more sustainable living than slash-and-burn farming and logging, which require people to move after destroying the crop. Today there are butterfly farms all over the world. Just visit on-line auction sites and search for "butterflies." You'll find farm-raised specimens from Florida, Latin America, Africa, Australia, and New Guinea.

In some cases, butterfly merchants simply collect specimens from natural habitats. Biologists have found that it is very difficult to overcollect all but the most colorful and valuable species. As their numbers decline, they become hard to find, and the next breeding cycle restores their numbers.

Some farmers plant host plants for the caterpillars of the species they want to collect. It is much easier to collect the eggs and rear the caterpillars and pupal cases in controlled, protected environments than to randomly search for caterpillars and pupae, and such an operation is much more profitable. In some cases, the entire farming operation takes place in a greenhouse or some other enclosure.

Butterflies and moths begin to lose their value to collectors within hours after emerging from their pupal cases. As soon as they begin to fly, their wings begin to tatter and show wear. Butterfly farmers monitor their crops and collect near-perfect adults immediately after mating. As most adult butterflies and moths die shortly after breeding, collecting adults after they mate is simply maximizing the value of a renewable resource.

All officially endangered species are protected by U.S. federal law, regardless of their origin. Reputable insect dealers have permits and licenses and never attempt to deal in endangered species. If you decide to support butterfly farming with purchases, beware of any source that offers endangered species; report such cases to your state wildlife agency or the U.S. Fish and Wildlife Service.

Butterfly farming is an innovative conservation technique that protects habitat, eliminates the need for poaching, promotes reproduction of the crop, provides a sought-after product to consumers, and generates a reasonable financial return to the farmers.

# CHAPTER 6

# Enjoying Butterflies

Once upon a time, it seems like a lifetime ago, before computer games, before the Cartoon Network, and before children's spare time was more tightly scheduled than their parents', there was a little boy in southeastern Pennsylvania who couldn't step outdoors without trying to catch everything that moved. Butterflies were particularly challenging, for obvious reasons. So his mother sewed a bag of cheesecloth around a coat hanger shaped into a hoop, and fastened it to the end of an old broomstick. Now he could run and jump across hayfields, pastures, and cemeteries to capture at least a few of the butterflies he had only been able to glimpse from afar. I was that little boy, though I'm certain many middle-aged baby boomers could tell similar tales of collecting butterflies in summer fields of fragrant flowers.

I learned as I went, thanks in large measure to a dog-eared copy of an early edition of Golden Press's *Butterflies and Moths: A Guide to the More Common American Species*. Not every butterfly I caught survived the ordeal, but I learned quickly about the importance of the powdery scales that covered my hands, and to handle these insects with a firm but gentle touch.

That's how many butterfly lovers came to be—through self-taught, firsthand experience.

Today the world's a different place. Kids have so many activities and an endless supply of increasingly fascinating toys competing for their attention that few of them have many outdoor experiences unless they belong to a 4-H club or attend nature camp. So it's up to parents, grandparents, and teachers to instill in children the wonder and appreciation of nature. Because insects, including butterflies and moths, are so common and widespread, they are the ideal creatures to capture kids' imagination.

## COLLECTING

Most kids learn best through hands-on experience, and the best way to learn about butterflies is to collect them. Years ago, many amateur naturalists maintained impressive butterfly collections that required killing and preparing captured specimens. And my advanced high school biology class required an insect collection. But that's not what I'm suggesting. As a society and culture, we've moved beyond valuing personal collections of natural artifacts. That's the business of museums, and they do it very well.

What I'm suggesting here is that kids maintain a temporary living collection. Capture butterflies, examine them, study them, try to identify them, then release them. Rather than keep boxes of dead, pinned butterflies and moths, record each species as a mark on a checklist or in a field guide. I keep my bird list in my favorite field guide, where I detail my observations, writing my notes next to the text, and I log butterfly observations the same way. Many states publish checklists of the most common species, and these lists are free for the asking. Some butterfly conservation organizations also offer checklists. Or in this age of computerized information, you can make your own list for your backyard, county, state, and/or region.

The beauty of butterfly collecting is that it's easy and requires minimal equipment. A good, fine-mesh aerial net is essential. These are available from biological supply houses (see Appendix D). A pair of flat-tipped forceps comes in handy for handling butterflies. And a four- or eight-power hand lens brings out the details of butterflies' colorful scales and anatomy.

## WATCHING

Over the last thirty years, bird-watching has emerged as a popular American pastime. More than 60 million Americans enjoy backyard birds. Most birds are active by day, colorful, and fun to watch. The same can be said for butterflies. And butterfly-watching is rapidly becoming a part of popular natural history culture.

The birth of the bird-watching boom can be traced to the publication of Roger Tory Peterson's first edition of *A Field Guide to Birds* in 1934. Though there have been field guides to butterflies available for decades, none seemed to capture the public's imagination the way the Peterson bird guide did. That changed in 1993 with the publication of *Butterflies through Binoculars: A Field Guide to Butterflies in the Boston, New York, Washington Region*, by Jeffrey Glassberg. The success of his subsequent titles, *Butterflies through Binoculars: A Field Guide to the Butterflies of Eastern North America* (1999), *Butterflies through Binoculars: A Field, Finding, and Gardening Guide to Butterflies in Florida* (2000), and *Butterflies through Binoculars: A Field Guide to the Butterflies of Western North America* (2001), confirms the trend.

Until Glassberg's books, all but the most common and familiar butterflies had to be captured and killed to be identified. That approach just didn't appeal to curious amateur naturalists who didn't want to destroy life in order to enjoy nature. Glassberg's approach revolutionized our approach to enjoying butterflies and may have introduced the notion of butterfly-watching.

Chasing butterflies for a good look is, as I learned as a little boy, a frustrating experience. Though they often perch to sip nectar or rest, they fly rapidly and erratically when approached too closely. Binoculars are the perfect solution. Just as they allow close inspection of birds from afar, binoculars allow you to see butterflies in great detail while they perch. With quality optics, you can enjoy their spectacular colors and patterns, and sometimes you can even detect the texture of the scales that cover their bodies.

Good birding binoculars will serve butterfly-watchers well, though they should have the ability to focus closely, as it's easy to approach within 8 to 10 feet of butterflies. Look for optics with "close-focus" capability when shopping for butterfly-watching binoculars.

Otherwise, 7x35 or 8x42 binoculars will serve butterfly-watchers well. The first number refers to the lens's magnifying power; eight-power binoculars make objects appear eight times closer than they really are. The second number is the diameter of the objective lenses (the ones farther from the eyes) in millimeters. The larger the objective lenses, the more light they transmit, and hence the brighter the image you see.

Optics are one of those products where you get what you pay for. Acceptable binoculars can be purchased for $200, but you can spend more than $1,000 for the finest optics. It's better to save for a while and buy better binoculars than to purchase an inexpensive pair that will get knocked out of alignment the first time you drop them. That causes the images seen through the two tubes to be slightly offset, and nothing is more frustrating to a nature-watcher. Better, more expensive brands come with lengthy or even lifetime warranties that cover this common problem. Repairing cheaper binoculars can cost more than the original purchase price. Bushnell, Nikon, Swarovski, Swift, Leica, and Zeiss are among the better brands of optics, and most have models in a range of prices. You'll find the best prices through mail-order and Internet supply houses, such as Eagle Optics in Middleton, Wisconsin (www.eagleoptics.com or 800-289-1132). Check birding and photography magazines for currents ads, prices, and contact information.

The actual act of watching butterflies is pretty simple. Just find an unmown park, old field, cemetery, or seldom traveled country road. You can walk in search of butterflies, or sit on a high spot and let them come to you. Either style can be rewarding.

An important aspect of any type of nature study is to record field notes. Amateur naturalists make vast numbers of observations and have made meaningful contributions to many areas of natural history. Taking field notes is one of the most important things we do. Record your observations. Historically, pen and paper were every keen observer's primary tools. Today modern technology—computers, sophisticated optics, and audio and video recorders—allows both amateur and professional biologists to process and organize information in ways that early naturalists could not have even imagined. Field notes, regardless of how they are recorded, have been and will continue to be the backbone of natural history.

But biological record keeping need not be high-tech. For most, it begins simply enough. After a few years of enjoying nature in the backyard, you realize the value of year-to-year comparisons. Maybe it's just a list on the refrigerator or scribbled notes on the calendar. Eventually, however, you buy a small notebook, and soon you find yourself taking notes on a weekly or even daily basis. You appreciate the value of your thoughts and observations, so you record them. Simply describe what you see. If words fail, draw a picture. Even stick figures with lines pointing to key features are helpful.

Field notes are a permanent record of your observations. Treat them as such. Use permanent ink that won't smear when wet. They are, after all, field notes. Get in the habit of recording a standard set of information for each entry: date, time, weather conditions, and a detailed description of the location. Describe new or hard-to-find places in detail so that even a stranger could find it from your description.

One need not be a skilled writer to keep field notes, so encourage children to keep field notes too. It will hone their powers of observation, teach them patience, and improve their writing skills.

A field journal is personal, so keep notes informal. Be brief. Write in phrases. Abbreviate. Don't worry about grammar or spelling. But keep notes legible and be clear enough that others might someday understand your message.

A typical entry might read: "6 April 1992; 2 pm; clr sky, about 60 degrees; driveway at house, near Cameron, Marshall Co., West Virginia; unfamiliar butterfly or perhaps day-flying moth; small, about one-inch wingspan; uniformly dark with large cream-colored patches on front wings and bright red patches on hind wings; check field guide later."

It turned out to be a Grapevine Epimenis (*Psychomorpha epimenis*). The field guide described it as "a woodland day-flier, often mistaken for a butterfly." My hunch was right, but without my notes, I probably would have forgotten about this little gem and never learned its name. Because I had my notes, I enjoyed the satisfaction of identifying a species I had never seen before.

Field notes help me recall what I've seen in years past, and more importantly, they signal what I should look for in the future. I can compare events from year to year and even decade to decade.

Field notes also add a fascinating dimension to travel of any sort. Doug Henry, a Pennsylvania science teacher I met in Wyoming a few years ago, keeps a journal whenever he travels. "I do it religiously," he told me. "Reviewing my journal lets me relive each trip. Even a single phrase can trigger a whole sequence of events in my mind that otherwise I'd forget."

Keeping field notes also helps you become a better nature-watcher. You learn to pay attention to detail. It fine-tunes your powers of observation. After you begin keeping field notes, you'll find yourself referring to them regularly.

Did you see any Mourning Cloaks in January this year? It's in your notebook.

When does butterfly milkweed begin blooming? Check your notebook to see when flowers appeared the last few years.

When did the first wave of migrating Monarchs move through last fall? Check your notes.

Whether they are handwritten accounts, computerized entries, photographs, drawings, or audiotapes, keeping records of the way things are may be the best way to protect the future of your favorite natural areas. Field notes are every naturalist's legacy, a great way to give something back to the natural world we spend a lifetime knowing and loving. Imagine if you had a notebook kept by your grandparents of the butterflies they saw on the old family farm. That's the value of field notes. That's the value of watching.

## PHOTOGRAPHY

Nature photography is one of the fastest-growing forms of outdoor recreation. Wherever nature-watchers gather, 35-millimeter and digital cameras and telephoto lenses abound.

But after investing hundreds or even thousands of dollars in expensive equipment, many aspiring wildlife photographers give up in frustration. Those full-frame portraits we all admire in wildlife books and magazines require more than just expensive equipment. Time, patience, and an understanding of the natural history of the subject are all critical. But there are a few tricks of the trade that can help you produce terrific photos in almost any backyard setting.

How do photographers get their subjects to cooperate for those beautiful portraits of butterflies on isolated flowers? All it requires is a basic understanding of butterfly behavior. Butterflies return repeatedly to favorite flower patches and even favorite flowers. Nectar-bearing flowers produce nectar almost continually, so as long as the flower blooms, nectar is available. Butterflies return to these flowers day after day. Find and study these flower patches, and learn which areas attract the most butterflies. Then set up a camera with a telephoto or close-up lens and a cable release on a tripod (essential for razor-sharp images), and prefocus on a popular flower. That's your complete outdoor "studio."

If there are any distractions in the background, move them. A colorful piece of a swing set or a jungle gym can ruin an otherwise memorable image. A blurred green or brown background, on the other hand, directs a viewer's attention to the photo's subject.

Now you're ready to shoot. Every time a butterfly lands on the perch, fire away. A motor drive enables you to get several exposures of each butterfly.

You'll quickly discover that it's easy to burn a lot of film in a hurry. Compared with the time, effort, and planning required to get good photos, however, film is cheap. If you get one or two keepers from each roll of film, congratulate yourself. Of course, if you've graduated to a digital camera you won't need any film at all.

Great photos reflect a combination of skill, patience, luck, and knowledge. Skill comes with experience. Patience comes from within. Luck is totally unpredictable. And with study comes knowledge.

## ZOOS

As the popularity of butterflies has grown in recent years, so have opportunities to see them in enclosed settings. Some zoos, museums, arboretums, and conservatories have butterfly houses. Some are permanent displays; others are billed as temporary, though if they prove popular, their status may change. Some butterfly farms in Florida have opened their doors to visitors. And some butterfly houses stand on their own. Because this is a developing attraction, conduct Internet searches on "butterfly farming" for current information.

Visiting a butterfly house is unlike a typical zoo experience. Visitors enter the large butterfly enclosure and walk right among the butterflies. They sometimes actually land on you, and signs warn to check your back for hitchhikers before leaving. Can you imagine a better way to spark a kid's interest in butterflies and nature?

If you prefer seeing free-flying butterflies in their natural habitat, visit state parks, nature centers, and other natural areas. Many have established butterfly gardens and meadows to attract a wide variety of local species.

# Nectar-Producing Plants

| Common Name | Scientific Name |
| --- | --- |
| Yarrow | *Achillea millefolium* |
| Dutchman's Pipe | *Aristolochia macrophylla* |
| Butterfly Weed | *Asclepias tuberosa* |
| Swamp Milkweed | *Asclepias incarnata* |
| Common Milkweed | *Asclepias syriaca* |
| Asters | *Aster* spp. |
| Indian Paintbrush | *Castilleja coccinea* |
| Turtlehead | *Chelone glabra* |
| Daisies | *Chrysanthemum* spp. |
| Thistle | *Cirsium* spp. |
| Cosmos | *Cosmos* spp. |
| Purple Coneflower | *Echinacea purpurea* |
| Joe-Pye Weed | *Eupatorium* spp. |
| Indian Blanket | *Gaillardia pulchella* |
| Sneezeweed | *Helenium autumnale* |
| Sunflowers | *Helianthus* spp. |
| Lantana | *Lantana* spp. |
| Blazing Star | *Liatris* spp. |
| Cardinal Flower | *Lobelia cardinalis* |
| Trumpet Honeysuckle | *Lonicera sempervirens* |
| Bluebonnet | *Lupinus subcarnosus* |
| Bee Balm | *Monarda didyma* |
| Bergamot | *Monarda media* |
| Phlox | *Phlox* spp. |
| Mesquite | *Prosopis juliflora* |
| Black Cherry | *Prunus serotina* |
| Black-Eyed Susan | *Rudbeckia hirta* |
| Salvia | *Salvia* spp. |
| Goldenrod | *Solidago* spp. |
| Ironweed | *Vernonia noveboracensis* |

# Caterpillar Food Plants

| Butterflies | Important Larval Food Plants |
|---|---|
| Tiger Swallowtail | Tulip poplar, black cherry, ash, spicebush |
| Spicebush Swallowtail | Spicebush, sassafras |
| Zebra Swallowtail | Pawpaw |
| Giant Swallowtail | Orange and other citrus species |
| Black Swallowtail | Parsley, dill, celery |
| Sulphurs and Whites | Legumes and mustards |
| Monarch | Milkweed |
| Satyrs and Wood Nymph | Various grasses |
| Viceroy | Willow, poplar, aspen, apple, cherry, plum |
| Red Admiral | Nettles |
| Painted Lady | Composites, legumes, nettles |
| American Painted Lady | Pussytoes, nettles, thistle |
| Question Mark and Comma | Elm, hackberry, nettles |
| Baltimore | Turtlehead |
| Buckeye | Plantains, snapdragons |
| Mourning Cloak | Willow, elm, poplar, birch |
| Fritillaries | Violets |
| Crescents | Asters |
| Red-Spotted Purple | Cherry, apple, aspen, oak, willow, hawthorn |
| Skippers | Various legumes |

| Moths | Important Larval Food Plants |
|---|---|
| Hawk Moth | Viburnum, apple, cherry, tomato, tobacco |
| Luna | Hickory, cherry, beech, willow, sweet gum, persimmon |
| Cecropia | Ash, apple, beech, elm, maple, oak, willow |
| Polyphemus | Ash, grape, maple, hickory, oak, pine, apple |
| Royal Walnut | Walnut, sumac, persimmon, lilac, ash, hickory, sycamore |
| Io | Redbud, maple, hackberry, cherry, corn, oak, sassafras |

# Invasive Exotic Plants to Avoid

## Grasses

| | |
|---|---|
| Cheatgrass | *Bromus tectorum* |
| Reed Canary Grass | *Phalaris arundinacea* |
| Johnson Grass | *Sorghum halepense* |
| Shattercane | *Sorghum bicolor* |
| Japanese Stilt Grass | *Microstegium vimineum* |
| Common Reed | *Phragmites australis* |

## Herbaceous species

| | |
|---|---|
| Purple Loosestrife | *Lythrum salicaria* |
| Canada Thistle | *Cirsium arvense* |
| Bull Thistle | *Cirsium vulgare* |
| Jimsonweed | *Datura stramonium* |
| Japanese Knotweed | *Polygonum cuspidatum* |
| Wild Parsnip | *Pastinaca sativa* |

## Vines

| | |
|---|---|
| Kudzu | *Pueraria lobata* |
| Oriental Bittersweet | *Celastrus orbiculatus* |
| Japanese Honeysuckle | *Lonicera japonica* |
| Mile-a-Minute Vine | *Polygonum perfoliatum* |

## Shrubs

| | |
|---|---|
| Autumn Olive | *Elaeagnus umbellata* |
| Russian Olive | *Elaeagnus angustifolia* |
| Amur Honeysuckle | *Lonicera maackii* |
| Morrow's Honeysuckle | *Lonicera morrowii* |
| Standish Honeysuckle | *Lonicera standishii* |
| Tatarian Honeysuckle | *Lonicera tatarica* |
| Multiflora Rose | *Rosa multiflora* |

*Note:* Butterfly Bush (*Buddleia* spp.) is widely touted as a butterfly magnet, and butterflies do swarm it for nectar, but it is not native to North America, and some ecologists worry that it could become invasive over time. Once again, my advice is "Go native!"

# Supply Houses for Collecting and Rearing Equipment

Fisher Science Education
485 S. Frontage Rd.
Burr Ridge, IL 60521
800-955-1177
www.fisheredu.com

Bio Quip
17803 LaSalle Ave.
Gardena, CA 90248-3602
310-324-0620
www.bioquip.com

Carolina Biological Supply
2700 York Rd.
Burlington, NC 27215
800-227-1150
www.carolina.com

Insect Lore Products
P.O. Box 1535
Shafter, CA 93263
800-LIVE-BUG

Ward's Natural Sciences
Establishment
P.O. Box 92912
Rochester, NY 14692
800-962-2660

# Membership Organizations

Xerces Society
4828 S.E. Hawthorne Blvd.
Portland, OR 97215
*Promotes biodiversity through
conservation of invertebrates*

North American Butterfly
Association
4 Delaware Rd.
Morristown, NJ 07960

Monarch Watch
University of Kansas
Entomology Program
1200 Sunnyside Avenue
Lawrence, KS 66045

Monarch Program
P.O. Box 178671
San Diego, CA 92177

Young Entomologists' Society
1915 Peggy Place
Lansing, MI 48910

Butterfly Gardeners'
Association
1021 N. Main St.
Allentown, PA 18104

Lepidoptera Research
Foundation
9620 Heather Rd.
Beverly Hills, CA 90210

Lepidopterists' Society
1900 John St.
Manhattan Beach, CA 90266

# Further Reading and Information Sources

Glassberg, J. 1995. *Enjoying Butterflies More.* Marietta, OH: Bird Watcher's Digest Press. 33 pp.

Halpern S. 2001. *Four Wings and a Prayer: Caught in the Mystery of the Monarch Butterfly.* New York: Pantheon Books. 212 pp.

Heitzman, J. R., and J. E. Heitzman. 1987. *Butterflies and Moths of Missouri.* Jefferson City: Missouri Department of Conservation. 385 pp.

Himmelman, J. 2002. *Discovering Moths: Nighttime Jewels in Your Own Backyard.* Camden, ME: Down East Books. 232 pp.

Leverton, R. 2001. *Enjoying Moths.* London: T. & A. D. Poyser. 276 pp.

Marinell, J. (ed.) 1996. *Going Native: Biodiversity in Our Own Backyards.* Handbook #140. New York: Brooklyn Botanic Garden. 112 pp.

Mikula, R. 1997. *Garden Butterflies of North America: A Gallery of Garden Butterflies and How to Attract Them.* Minocqua, WI: Willow Creek Press. 143 pp.

Mikula, R. 2000. *The Family Butterfly Book: Projects, Activities, and a Field Guide to 40 Favorite North American Species.* Pownal, VT: Storey Books, 166 pp.

New, T. R. 1991. *Butterfly Conservation.* New York: Oxford University Press. 224 pp.

Opler, P. A., and G. O. Krizek. 1984. *Butterflies East of the Great Plains.* Baltimore: Johns Hopkins University Press. 294 pp.

Pyle, R. M. 1984. *Handbook for Butterfly Watchers.* Boston: Houghton Mifflin. 280 pp.

Pyle, R. M. 1999. *Chasing Monarchs: Migrating with the Butterflies of Passage.* Boston: Houghton Mifflin. 307 pp.

Schappert, P. 2000. *A World for Butterflies: Their Lives, Behavior, and Future.* Buffalo, NY: Firefly Books. 320 pp.

Scott, J. A. 1986. *The Butterflies of North America: A Natural History and Field Guide*. Stanford, CA: Stanford University Press. 583 pp.

Shull, E. M. 1987. *The Butterflies of Indiana*. Bloomington: Indiana University Press. 262 pp.

Tekulsky, M. 1985. *The Butterfly Garden: Turning Your Garden, Window Box or Backyard into a Beautiful Home for Butterflies*. Boston: Harvard Common Press. 144 pp.

Tuskes, P. M., J. P. Tuttle, and M. M. Collins. 1996. *The Wild Silk Moths of North America*. Ithaca, NY: Cornell University Press. 250 pp.

Xerces Society. 1998. *Butterfly Gardening: Creating Summer Magic in Your Garden*. Revised ed. San Francisco: Sierra Club Books. 208 pp.

Young, M. 1997. *The Natural History of Moths*. London: T. & A. D. Poyser. 271 pp.

## FIELD GUIDES

Allen, T. 1997. *The Butterflies of West Virginia and Their Caterpillars*. Pittsburgh: University of Pittsburgh Press. 388 pp.

Covell, C. V., Jr. 1984. *A Field Guide to the Moths of Eastern North America*. Boston: Houghton Mifflin. 496 pp.

Glassberg, J. 1993. *Butterflies through Binoculars: A Field Guide to Butterflies in the Boston, New York, Washington Region*. New York: Oxford University Press.

Glassberg, J. 1999. *Butterflies through Binoculars: A Field Guide to the Butterflies of Eastern North America*. New York: Oxford University Press. 242 pp.

Glassberg, J. 2001. *Butterflies through Binoculars: A Field Guide to the Butterflies of Western North America*. New York: Oxford University Press. 374 pp.

Glassberg, J., M. C. Minno, and J. V. Calhoun. 2001. *Butterflies through Binoculars: A Field, Finding, and Gardening Guide to Butterflies in Florida*. New York: Oxford University Press. 242 pp.

Mitchell, R. T., and H. S. Zim. 1987. *Butterflies and Moths: A Guide to the More Common American Species*. New York: Golden Press. 160 pp.

Opler, P. A. 1994. *Peterson First Guide to Butterflies and Moths*. Boston: Houghton Mifflin. 128 pp.

Opler, P. A., and V. Malikul. 1992. *A Field Guide to Eastern Butterflies*. Boston: Houghton Mifflin. 396 pp.

Wagner, D. L., V. Giles, R. C. Reardon, and M. L. McManus. 1997. *Caterpillars of Eastern Forests*. FHTET-96-34. Morgantown, WV: USDA. 113 pp.

Wright, A. B. 1993. *Peterson First Guide to Caterpillars of North America*. Boston: Houghton Mifflin. 128 pp.

## WEBSITES

www.butterflyalphabet.com
www.monarchwatch.org
www.arthropod.net
www.billsbutterflies.com
www.boneroom.com
www.npsc.nbs.gov/resource/distr/lepid/bflyusa/bflyusa.htm
www.npsc.nbs.gov/resource/distr/lepid/moths/mothsusa.htm
www.xerces.org
www.naba.org

# Index of Species